# The Documentary Makers

**David A Goldsmith**

Interviews with 15 of
the Best in the Business

RotoVision

A RotoVision Book
Published and distributed by RotoVision SA
Route Suisse 9
CH-1295 Mies
Switzerland

RotoVision SA
Sales, Editorial & Production Office
Sheridan House, 112/116A Western Road
Hove, East Sussex BN3 1DD, UK

T +44 (0)1273 72 72 68
F +44 (0)1273 72 72 69
E sales@rotovision.com
www.rotovision.com

10 9 8 7 6 5 4 3 2 1

ISBN 2-88046-730-6

Book design by Rose Design

Production and separations by
Hong Kong Scanner Arts, China

Printing by Midas Printing, China

The documentary...
00:00:06

01
**Ken Burns, USA**
00:00:08

02
**Molly Dineen, UK**
00:00:20

03
**Alastair Fothergill, UK**
00:00:32

04
**Hans-Dieter Grabe, Germany**
00:00:44

05
**Patricio Guzmán, Chile**
00:00:54

06
**Bonnie Sherr Klein, Canada**
00:00:64

07
**Barbara Kopple, USA**
00:00:74

08
**Jørgen Leth, Denmark**
00:00:86

# Contents

# The documentary...

is as old as cinema itself; and is accepted, often inventive, and frequently provocative. It commands serious investment, is capable of attracting respectable-size audiences and being sold around the world. While the television documentary flourishes, that of its cinema cousin has been relegated to the cine-tech and cine-club.

Of all television forms—entertainment, current affairs, drama, sport—the one least clearly defined and most open to interpretation is the documentary. The question as to what is, and what is not, a documentary is continually challenged. Whatever the current definition, there exists an unwritten agreement between maker and audience that the content be factual. From there to the world of fiction lies a minefield of variation and interpretation, through which the documentary maker must tread with care and integrity, and the viewer must pass with tolerance and respect. The former is required to be inventive and original in the handling of the subject matter, yet honoring the principles of good journalism without recourse to exaggeration or insupportable claims. For the latter, there needs be a willingness to go along with the spirit of enquiry, to allow a case to be presented without rushing to judgement, and a readiness to

consider alternative and conflicting viewpoints. Having struck such a balance, the power and the value of the documentary can be elevating, informative, and entertaining as no other area of the medium is capable of achieving. But the rules of engagement for the makers of documentaries are various and complicated. They are prone to inhibiting factors varying from country to country, culture to culture—laws of libel and privacy on the one hand, the public's right to know and freedom of the press on the other, for what is deemed offensive in one country might well be commonplace in a neighboring one.

Having found an acceptable definition of "documentary," if only by exclusion, what prerequisites does the documentary maker require? Well, having an eye for a story, a way with people, and the charisma to lead, are some of the qualities needed. Also to know the tools of their trade, and increasingly nowadays, an ability to use them. So the documentary director will need to be both architect and artisan. And then to have a journalistic bent. Journalistic in that the documentary maker needs to apply the same rigorous standards to the business of collating data, reporting facts, eliciting alternative viewpoints as any serious correspondent of the press. It is held that the documentary has to tell a story, but with a level of insight above and beyond its mere telling; it is not sufficient to re-tell an episode in the life of the person featured or social issue under discussion, but to explain and justify the background and circumstance that gave rise to the events truthfully and accurately. The documentary is, after all, intended to inform, sometimes to motivate, but also to entertain as it competes for time and space with all program forms.

A glance at the brief history of the moving image shows the documentary to have been in at the birth. The desire to document images led to the development of the film camera so as to better understand what constitutes movement—for the Frenchman, Pierre Jules César Janssen, it was the eclipse of the sun by the planet Venus in 1874; for the Englishman, Eadweard Muybridge, some six years later, it was the need to analyze the gallop of the race-horse. Then came an intense commercial competition to develop the film camera, a competition led by the American Thomas Alva Edison and the Frenchman Louis Lumière during the final years of the 1800s. For his part, Lumière foresaw the future of the cinema and captured the great sights of nature and Man's invention. He introduced the world to everyday life, fascinating audiences with scenes of themselves at work and play, even frightening them with the commonplace such as the locomotive arriving at La Ciotat, in southern France. His "*operateurs*" filmed and projected their work before audiences in Australia and Europe, the Middle East and Indochina, North and South America. And so the world was introduced to "actuality." The rest, as they say, is history. And it is the most recent history with which we are occupied in this book. The documentary makers presented here represent the period in which the documentary has become an established and commonplace form received within the privacy of the home.

The degree to which the documentary reflects reality, truth, actuality, call it what you will, remains an open issue. Camera angles and edit points are carefully selected for reasons of continuity or effect—seemingly natural, yet highly contrived. The contributors to this book have sought to strike a balance between their desire to present fact (as they see it) with the art of storytelling. They are all too familiar with the power of the moving image, the emotion generated by use of sound, pace, and composition. They know how to manipulate these elements so as to carry an audience with them, and they know, when mishandled, how the same elements will alienate and destroy the purpose of their work. The criteria for selecting the filmmakers for this book has not been easy—simply a selection of the few from the many who have arguably advanced the state of the art.

The history of the television documentary is one shaped by technology—from celluloid to video, from black and white to color, from analog to digital, from linear to non-linear, from the scarcity of terrestrial broadcast spectrum to the plethora of satellite, cable, and digital transmission. With each new era came a new approach to the making of the documentary. And with each advance came a new set of challenges for documentary makers—artistic, moral, political, religious, social. But regardless of background, creed, or color, all documentary makers have in common their search of an audience. Television has delivered, now the documentary makers must feed the beast with a diet that is entertainingly varied, provocatively stimulating, and intellectually nutritious.

*Varese, 2003*

# Ken
# Burns

# 01

### An introduction

It is said that more Americans got to know their history from the films of Ken Burns than from any other source. Burns has mastered the technique of bringing the archives to life in such series as *The Civil War, Baseball,* and *Jazz, A History of America's Music.* Thanks to Ken Burns and his team, in excess of 50 million American viewers have seen, heard, and felt the pulse of their short history. "Given 10,000 years," he says, "I would never run out of ideas on American history."

# Ken Burns

*New Hampshire, December 8, 2002*

My very first memory is of playing in my father's darkroom, but the most important event in my life was in 1965 when my mother, who had been diagnosed with cancer, passed away after ten years of intense suffering for her—and our family. I think my mother's illness formed a deep psychological urge in me to delve into history.

History is malleable, the facts are not. History is the questions we, in the present, ask of the past. There is a good deal in my adult psychology that is searching the past for some sort of healing.

In a sense, I've made the same film over and over again, each film asking the same deceptively simple question: "Who are we? What does the past tell us about those strange and complicated people who like to call themselves Americans?" The question, while never ever answered, only deepens with each film, and mutates and transforms into "Who am I?" It all goes back to being a little boy, watching my mother die and at the same time seeing on television fire hoses and police dogs turned on black protestors in the South during the early '60s. Somehow the cancer that was killing my country helped to mitigate the cancer that was killing my family.

After my mother died, my father kept me on a fairly strict curfew, relaxed only when there was an old movie on television or at the university cinema guild, which showed old and New Wave films that were blossoming in the early to mid '60s. The first time I'd ever seen my father cry was at old movies, and this was both terrifying and extremely provocative; I found myself inextricably drawn to filmmaking as a way of life.

I was born in Brooklyn, New York, in 1953. My mother was a biological technician and my father an anthropologist whose area of study was Alpine peasants. I soon left New York City and went with my parents to Saint Véran, the highest village in Europe, and spent my first year there, and then returned to the US. Though I have no memories of that year, the photographs that memorialized the trip and its powerful symbolism for our whole family ensured that I would keep the experience, however outwardly unremembered, a part of my make-up as I grew up.

By 1971, I thought I would be a feature filmmaker like Hitchcock, Hawks, or more particularly, Ford, who seemed to be singing, in Homeric fashion, the epic verses of American history. At this stage I was completely untrained and untutored in American history, besides that forced down my throat in high school. I attended Hampshire College in Amherst, Massachusetts, where I studied under Jerome Liebling and Elaine Mayes, social-documentary still photographers, who responded to my interest in feature films with a shrug of their shoulders, and reminded me how much drama there is in "what is" and "what was." That set me completely on end. They were mentors who imparted not just the techniques of filmmaking and photography, but some larger ethos that has permeated my work ever since. I left Hampshire in 1975 wanting to be a documentary filmmaker. Of the 70-odd students drawn to film our first year, only three or four of us graduated in film, and we are still making films.

For my final fourth-year project I tested the historical waters, so to speak, with a half-hour documentary about agricultural communities in late 18th- to early 19th-century America called *Working in Rural New England*. I felt I had found my life's work. Liebling and Mayes taught not just the history and appreciation of photography and, by extension, documentary, but a broad humanistic tradition in which history and ethical responsibility go hand in hand with filmmaking. I discovered a latent interest in history that provided me with subject matter for the next 30 years. I also learned how to remove myself from the process, and how to respect the power of the single image to convey complex information without undue manipulation, because we had been so rooted in still photography. It seems a natural relative of filmmaking, but is often not. I know of only a few other instances where film and photography are taught together. For Liebling and Mayes, the constituent building blocks of cinema were the single photographic image, and so documentary films, which often mindlessly excused the scratchy, blurry, "out of focus," and badly framed, were not tolerated. (Others of honest energy, however flawed technically, were embraced.)

*Brooklyn Bridge*, 1981

I started my company, Florentine Films, with fellow Hampshire graduates Roger Sherman and Buddy Squires. Our first documentary dealt with the building and symbolism of the Brooklyn Bridge. Amy Stechler, who came into the company as we began work on this project, became a writer and editor and the woman I was to marry. We are now divorced, but she worked with me for a couple more films before the birth of our children convinced her to stay home and raise them. We moved to this tiny little village over 24 years ago because I needed to go to a place where I could live and work inexpensively. I was afraid that after I had shot my film on the Brooklyn Bridge I would have to get a real job in New York and might never return to editing that film. When you become a documentary filmmaker, you take a vow of anonymity and poverty. Fortunately, neither has happened. As it turned out, that first film, *Brooklyn Bridge*, was nominated for an Academy Award, and got a wonderful reception on the Public Broadcasting Service (PBS), igniting an interest in historical films not only from the PBS network, but from other US institutions such as schools and universities.

Now there are nine full-time employees in my company, although I am not one of them. I only get paid when grant money is provided—it keeps me working hard. At the height of editing a project like *Jazz*, our largest production, we had 40 people with five cutting rooms going in our editing house in New Hampshire. We do take unpaid interns from a couple of local colleges, and the ones who are most talented we later hire as apprentices, then assistants, then associates, and then full editors. So we have both new blood and people we've worked with for 20 years influencing all that is done here.

My films have a lot of words in them, which can create the mistaken idea that they are pre-planned and structured. We begin a project with a research period during which we delve into the subject, but not with a legion of researchers. In fact it's only a small coterie of us who work on it, including our writer. The writer and I work on a script without concern as to whether there are images to illustrate the script. At the same time my co-producers and I go into the field and begin shooting without any awareness of what's in the developing script. We are drawn, purely visually, to material in archives and in the field, to interviews with interesting people without concern about where that material might fit in the developing script. For a good deal of the process the left hand doesn't know what the right hand is doing. I will be constantly reading and suggesting script ideas to the writer and conferring with consultants and others on draft scripts. On the third or fourth draft, we finally go into the editing room to reconcile the mountain of visual evidence we have accumulated—re-photography of old photographs and paintings and other graphic material; the best comments from our interviews; and our live cinematography and other found footage such as newsreel and home movies. Inevitably there are scripted scenes for which there are no images, and often an abundance of visuals with no script. This is the advantage of not relying on a script as the god of the editing process— merely a guide of equal status with the visual material. Paul Strand, the great still photographer, insisted on this concept of "equivalence"; we employ it to forge a new relationship between word and image until the end of editing. I believe we are free of the problem of many documentaries, that of being an expression of an already arrived-at end, rather than being the expression of a joyous process of discovery.

Interviews are done without subjects' knowing the questions in advance, and never thinking that what they say might fit a certain spot in the script. I just follow the interviewees' trains of thought. This often helps to bring the past alive, and the placement of every interview select is always a happy accident of trial and error. When Wynton Marsalis in *Jazz* seemingly responds to a first-person historical quote that's in the film, viewers may think I played that quote to him just before he gave his answer. In fact, in every film the interviewee is just responding to a potentially unrelated question that becomes irrelevant once the interview bite is placed in the film. For example, at the very end of the first episode of *Jazz*, Wynton appears to respond to a quote by a white jazz musician named Nick LaRocca from the early '20s, taking credit for the invention of jazz, when over the previous 90 minutes we have learned that jazz came from the African American community. The first time I heard this quote was more than a year after I'd

Left: Writer Shelby Foote and Ken Burns (right)
*The Civil War*, 1990

Right: *The Civil War*, 1990

interviewed Wynton. I spent maybe six months editing before realizing that this interview select had to go in at this particular point, and it was perfect. It's a classic example of the way in which a talking head found a home. And we film live cinematography with a more painterly, two-dimensional relationship, looking for something relatively static in our work, the exact opposite of what you'd expect. We also record our music before editing, so it is as organic an element as the still photographs. Finally, the narration is made up of both first- and third-person voices.

In raising money for *Brooklyn Bridge*, funding sources required the finished film to be given to the PBS network for possible broadcast. It is such a labor-intensive, time-consuming process combing the archives, traveling the country, spending time in the editing room, and evolving the complex relationship between script and image, that I needed financial support from both corporations and charitable foundations to supplement government grants. The only attractive thing that I could offer in exchange for their support was a national showing on PBS. It was clear that I was going to have to trade the intimate communion between a cinema audience and a film for the much larger audience of television. Instead of reaching perhaps several thousand, from the very beginning we began to reach several million, and with *The Civil War* and *Baseball*, literally tens of millions—in the specific case of *Baseball*, upwards of 50 million. But of course it's still very difficult to raise the money.

Over the last 25 years, I've been able to make the films I've wanted to make, to choose the subjects myself, and to produce them free of interference from sponsors. Only colleagues and our scholarly board of advisors assembled for each production influence the outcome. I am also content to spend

an entire film in the pre-newsreel, pre-motion picture era. Newsreel of the great baseball hero, Babe Ruth, running around the bases, allows you to talk only about Babe Ruth running around the bases. But a photograph of Ruth's face allowed us to talk about his uneasy childhood, his difficulties with women and management, his later life—as well as his running around the bases.

When I shoot old photographs at various archives, I do not shoot them at arm's length. I might shoot 15 or 20 images within a single picture of, say, a Matthew Brady photograph in *The Civil War*, microscopically examining the landscape and trusting that the image is the closest record we have to a scene that was once very much alive. In addition to looking at the images, I listen to them as I re-photograph them. I know that sounds strange, but, looking at a Civil War photograph, I hear cannon firing, troops tramping across fields of battle. In *Jazz* I hear the sound of ice tinkling in glasses on a bar, people moving around the tables, and instruments tuning up; it all helps to create a greater degree of intimacy. For a good deal of *The Civil War*, and every film before that, animation stand (rostrum camera) work represented 1 or 2 percent of the visual material. The rest was the most primitive shooting arrangement you could possibly imagine—a piece of wood into which sheet metal is inserted and onto which, using magnets, photographs are mounted. The camera is moved in and out by hand. For *Brooklyn Bridge* we made a 90-second tilt-down on a newspaper headline, done by hand with careful follow-focus, using only two lamps bounced off umbrellas to disperse the light and keep the heat off the archives. In this way we have handled copies of the Declaration of Independence that were handwritten by Thomas Jefferson, and many other extraordinary documents—all very low tech, and shot in 16mm.

We have only just switched to computer editing, but I don't imagine ever changing to video from film. There is almost a romantic relationship that's there, and I don't like the feel of video. A painter deals with pigments of a cellular nature. A filmmaker, who works in a chemical and therefore a molecular process, gets to hold the film, cut it physically, hold it up to the light. Video is more abstract, electronic, a cosmology removed in which you never touch "the thing"; there's no, as Gertrude Stein said, "there, there." The reason I switched to computer editing is because the flatbed editing table was so anachronistic to the young people in my organization. Teaching them how to use a Steinbeck was like teaching a race-car driver how to shoe a horse. But I haven't thrown the flatbeds out, just put them in mothballs.

I consciously eschew the misguided consensus of many of my colleagues that film is the enemy of the word, and over more than a score of productions I have tried to celebrate the word as much as possible. I hope that what we have in our narration is a cogent and at times poetic evocation of the subject. The narration is refined and re-refined, thrown out, replaced, resurrected, and, in short, worked on continually from beginning to end. We supplement third-person narration with a chorus of first-person voices in most of our films, found in the course of our research, that represent the journals, love letters, diaries, newspaper accounts, or military records that we use. That permits the past to speak for itself in documentary fashion, coupled with the presence of on-camera witnesses as contributing commentary.

We do not pay interviewees for the obvious journalistic reason that we do not wish to be buying their testimony, the exception being some indigent individuals to whom we give a modest daily stipend.

Family dwelling, Pleasant Hill, Kentucky
*The Shakers: Hands to Work, Hearts to God*, 1984

Meeting room and dwelling,
Hancock, Massachusetts
*The Shakers: Hands to Work, Hearts to God*, 1984

Blacksmith's shop, Hancock
*The Shakers: Hands to Work, Hearts to God*, 1984

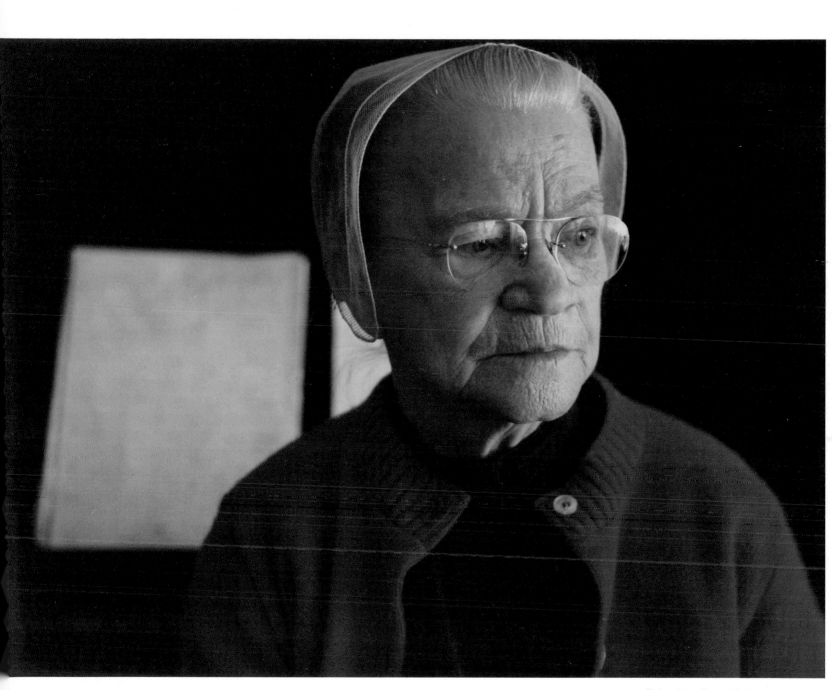

Shaker eldress Gertrude Soule
*The Shakers: Hands to Work, Hearts to God,*
1984

*Statue of Liberty*, 1985

Cinematographer Buddy Squires
on *Statue of Liberty*, 1985

There were several instances in *Jazz* when I declined to film individuals of renown because they requested payment. I felt that wasn't appropriate, given their stature and their financial well-being. As much as I felt the film could have benefited from their participation, I was disinclined to involve them at such an exorbitant price. So there are many ethical issues. God is objective. I am not. In the mere selection of historical facts I betray who I am, avoiding undue manipulation of facts to advocate anything political. We try to give a multi-dimensional view. In our arrangement of facts and in our use of imagery, we are constantly taking aesthetic and poetic license. I know this often raises ethical questions, and suggests borders across which we try not to step. But it is important to engage the possibilities of the medium fully—to go right up to the edge of those borders to serve a larger historical truth.

For example, my most celebrated film is the 11½ hour, nine-part history of the American Civil War. Hundreds of thousands of images were taken during the war, but not one of the 16,000 or 17,000 that I shot over 5½ years of production is of battle— because none exist. Back then, photographic equipment was too cumbersome, exposure times were too long, and the dangers were too great. In the episode on the Battle of Gettysburg, you see troops massed before battle and hear a cannon fire on a cut to the mouth of a cannon, but it is an

artillery piece from troops assembled before the battle. Then we have a cut to the dead on the battlefield taken after the battle to help suggest that the battle is raging. Three years before, when shooting in the National Archives in Washington, I found a detail of blurry leaves from the corner of one nondescript shot that I inserted in that scene to create the sense of confusion in battle. We squeeze the last bit of juice from these photographs to help tell a story. In *The Civil War* battles take 20 to 25 percent of the screen time, which means that whatever imagery I used is in essence poetic license, a lie. But we serve a larger truth in which the story wins out, but never so as to compromise the historical truth. And then there are the sound effects, which traditionally used to fade out when an interview came on in other films. This seemed to go against the grain of what I was trying to do in the Civil War film. I try to make these old photographs come alive with a first-person voice, cogent narration, and rich effects. I remember we stopped for almost a week and had violent arguments in the editing room about whether it was ethical to run effects under the interviews. Now, watching Shelby Foote describing the way Nathan Bedford Forrest escaped from the Battle of Shiloh, I think, and, more importantly, the audience feels, that he is actually there. It is so effective hearing the sounds of battle in the background. Another filmmaker might find this a violation, but I find it—and the question it raises—to be the most interesting part of what I do.

The future for our industry is beset by a number of problems; I think we're easily distracted in the documentary world by the so-called promises of the digital and internet revolution, the technological tail-of-the-dog wagging the dog. We need to refine good storytelling more than we need to get it fast. There is no democracy in art; the fact that anybody with a camera can become a filmmaker is true to one extent, but few will produce anything worthwhile. Documentary has no career path; everybody has to forge his or her own unique way. You have to be true to yourself, you've got to know that you have something to say, and you can be true to that voice which flickers at times and burns brighter at others. As Thomas Edison said of genius, "1 percent inspiration and 99 percent perspiration."

I remain passionately engaged with understanding the twin themes in America that distinguish us from European tradition—race and space—that is to say the physicality of the US in all its beauty and its ugliness. I'm constantly humbled by the complexity of human beings and their behavior, rejecting those who would reduce everything to black and white. The shades of gray I was taught in the darkroom were real lessons. Now, as a result of the popularity of my films, I've been wooed by Hollywood, but the constraints imposed by the system they call "the industry" are too industrial to tolerate, and I retreat to the artistic freedom I have with PBS.

Ken Burns at the American Philosophical
Society, Philadelphia
*Lewis and Clark*, 1997

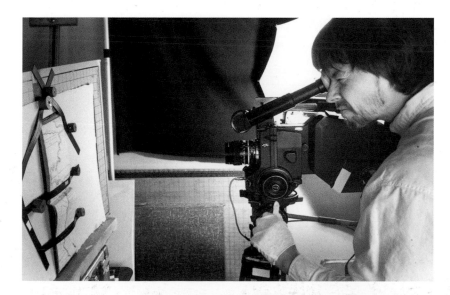

# Molly Dineen

02

## An introduction

Of Dineen it can be said, she is The Woman with the Movie Camera. From her first film about Jamaican sound systems, made while studying at the London College of Printing, to her recent *The Lords' Tale* for the UK's Channel Four, Dineen's ability to direct, shoot, and interview all at the same time mark her extraordinary ability. Her capacity to win the confidence and co-operation of her subjects is a testament to her exhaustive approach and fascination with eccentric institutions and humans. Mark Lawson in the Guardian newspaper observed, "A Dineen film tends to be positioned at the mid-point between a hug and a shove."

# Molly Dineen

*London, September 14, 2002*

I really do believe that nearly everyone is born with a natural talent and it's just a matter of luck whether it's harnessed or not. I've been lucky. Although I was born in Canada, I was brought up in England in Birmingham. People are always slagging off Birmingham, but actually it was fantastic. I was very happy there and I liked the scale of the town; even as schoolgirls my friends and I got to know artists, fashion designers, people starting up pop groups—there was a definite feeling of creativity in the time and the place.

Both my parents were totally supportive of me and my interests, so I didn't plod on in the smart girls' school where the teaching was lousy, where they read from a book and we wrote it down. I left as soon as I could and took myself off to the Bournville College of Art. Bournville has now amalgamated with other Midland colleges and universities to become the University of Middle England, the largest university in the country, and a few years ago they gave me a doctorate, which was lovely. Especially as the Dean of the Arts Faculty turned out to be my favorite Bournville teacher, the man who first interested me in photography.

I started doing a photography course at the London College of Printing (LCP), but moved quickly over to cinematography. My graduation film was a video called *Sound Business*, all about Jamaican sound systems, the guys who rap over backing tracks played by DJs in the clubs. It was quite dodgy then for a young white girl to hang around with a crowd of Jamaicans, but I stuck in there for so long that they eventually accepted me, and some of them became good friends. It taught me early on that you can't expect to just walk into a room with a camera and capture the truth about anybody or anything.

It was always the people that interested me, I was crap at the technical side. So what job did I get after leaving the LCP? A video camera crew assistant, changing all the plugs (usually incorrectly), setting up the machinery, lugging heavy equipment about. Video was beginning to be a sexy medium; suddenly everybody was shooting stuff on tape. This was techno broadcast land, but I loved the shoots, and although I hadn't a clue what I was

doing, even got to line up the cameras. I just copied this brilliant technical bloke who was part of the team. Then it got a bit sticky. I'd annoy the cameraman by asking him what he was going to shoot next, or I'd question the producers about the content of the piece—I got the sack.

I applied to the National Film School, which accepted me on the strength of my LCP film. Colin Young, the school's director, was deeply rooted in *cinema vérité*, so had a fundamental interest in documentary, which was then generally considered hippydom, and Herb Di Gioia ran the documentary side. Herb taught with passion and conviction. I remember him showing us a film shot of someone inside a car looking out and the next shot showing the car going by. Herb stopped the machine and shouted: "Can you believe it? Where's the eye supposed to be?" We were confused... surely that's how people tell stories? It was just one of the ways he succeeded in breaking down our expectation of how things should be put together. Herb taught us about fluidity, how to choreograph ourselves with the camera, how not to block a doorway or stop a person doing something, how to catch that part of their body or face that expresses mood or reaction. It was all about how you capture reality, not fragmenting it into shots to be cut together in the edit.

I wrote a shooting script for my first film which he read out mockingly to the class: "Long shot. Nuns up corridor to camera. Side shot. Nuns enter chamber." He tore me to pieces. But then, when Geoff Dunlop came to show us part of his Arab series Herb took the piss out of him, too. There were a lot of beautiful panning shots with music, and Herb pointed out how little that had to do with reality. Hence we shot from the hip like Don Pennebaker. That was when I started *Home From the Hill*, a film about a wonderfully eccentric elderly Colonel forced to leave his home in Kenya and return to England. Although I'd only just started at the school I knew I had to have a project, or I'd just hang out for seven years in turtleneck sweaters watching movies.

My boyfriend and I were going to Kenya that Christmas to stay with his father, so I thought

British Army in Northern Ireland
*In the Company of Men*, 1995

maybe my project could be about white colonials. I took a wind-up 16mm Bolex and a Beaulieu and a little sync-pulse tape recorder so I could shoot some reference stuff. By an extraordinary coincidence my boyfriend's father, Colonel Hook, was being evicted from the house where he'd lived for most of his life. I asked him if I could make a film about it, and he said, "Of course, sweetie," and it was the beginning of endless discussions, shootings, and screenings. The edit took a year— a bad precedent to have set myself. Will Wyatt came to the school around that time to tell us that none of us would get jobs. The next morning he phoned up wanting to buy my film, but said they needed to re-cut it. There was a terrible scene about that. I mean, a tired old drama director was given my film to put into shape. He moved the end to the beginning and cut important pauses out of interviews. When Colonel Hook said: "We made soldiers out of savages," you knew, from the way he said it, that it was self-parody, you could see it in his face. But this BBC director used that remark as voiceover to a shot of the old man sitting in an armchair surrounded by hovering African servants. There was a sweetness in Colonel Hook's relationship with his servants, but this edit made him out to be a didactic, racist, vile character. Yes, I was thrilled the BBC had bought my film, but I'd joined Herb's spiritual camp—I was extreme and purist about observational cinema. In the end they cut 12 minutes and ran it in the *40 Minutes* slot.

My mother had three children almost immediately after she got married and, 40 years on, impressed us all by getting a degree in French-Russian linguistics. My father got a scholarship to Cambridge, went into marketing, and ended up chairman of a large City financial services company. Neither of them had any experience in the arts world, but I'm sure the reason why my sister is a successful artist and I've made a name in documentary filmmaking is because, although they were divorced when I was seven, both parents united in backing us up in whatever we wanted to do. My stepmother, a newspaper journalist, has also been an incredibly strong influence on me. She got involved with the people she interviewed, like I do (strange people she'd written about would appear at the dinner table), and was fantastically principled about showing them her copy before it was printed.

My approach with participants is to say, "If you're willing to talk and let me film, I'll show you the material when it's in roughcut." I've always done that. In fact, I've been a bit anoraky about doing so, even for somebody who just appears briefly, but they don't get editorial control. Geri Halliwell was the exception; she's a pop star, and when I made *Geri*, a 90-minute portrait of her after she left the Spice Girls, she wanted total control. We settled on 50-50. I knew I'd never done a film she couldn't bear and suspected she'd quite enjoy seeing herself having a crisis. She cried when I screened the film.

I said: "My God, what's the matter?" and she said, "Oh, I just feel so sorry for me." She even gave me interviews sitting on the lavatory. She loved it. I honestly think there's a line with people you mustn't cross and you shouldn't try and catch them off their guard. She and I would go into the toilet because it was the only place to get away from the press. Actually, that was a big advantage of shooting DVCAM, she was very relaxed—it was very girlie between us.

Colonel Hook, in *Home from the Hill*, agreed to be filmed because he was lonely. There are always reasons why people say yes, and you have to be aware of why. With Colonel Hook there was genuine unhappiness about the loss of his wife and having to come back to the UK, but I never touched on that. "A great fat woman is what I want," he'd say, and I respected his privacy and kept within his chosen boundaries because the reality was too painful. If I hadn't I would have felt a sense of betrayal, and I think the viewer would, too.

During the making of *The Ark*, a film about London Zoo, I was aware that something dodgy was going on. Some large construction companies were on the Zoo's council and there was talk of partial closure and wanting to sell off part of the land for real estate. That would be a red rag to a bull for some filmmakers, but had I shown an interest in that aspect, the institution would have stopped

Geri Halliwell
*Geri*, 1999

Colonel Hilary Hook
*Home from the Hill*, 1985

trusting me. Also, if I included something sensational I'd find myself making a news story, not the documentary I was trying to do.

In the *40 Minutes* film, *Heart of the Angel*, about the psyche of the staff 300 feet down on the Angel Underground station, there were these three Irish workmen in the tunnels at night talking about being jockeys. Everything they talked about was green and light and colorful, and there they were in this black tunnel full of smoke and the flames of their Tilley lamps—a kind of heaven and hell. It's an absolute disgrace that the London Underground is still hand-swept with dustpan and brush by fluffers at night. I did think that if I put this in it might be out of line with the theme and mess up the whole texture of what I was trying to do. I also thought there'd be trouble if I showed it on film, but I got away with it on that one and it turned out to be the most popular, talked-about scene in the film.

Much of what was going on with the soldiers in making *In the Company of Men* would have been enormously juicy. One of the most riveting things about long-term residential regiments in Northern Ireland is the management of those blokes; the boredom factor, the drug factor, the chick factor, the way the men are with each other in their rooms. They are very physical, they dance together a lot. I'd have loved to have gone into all that, but I exercised self-censorship because I knew what the reaction would be if I went out with a bunch of army guys, they got drunk, picked up a load of chicks, and I shot it all. It would destroy the trust. The shoot the next morning on patrol was stronger because I'd been out with them all night without the camera, and the guy giving that bleary interview over the hedge was talking to a friend with a hangover, not thinking, "Oh, Jesus, she's a reporter."

In my latest film, *The Lords' Tale*, about the abolition—or part-abolition as it turned out—of hereditary peers, Channel Four expected it to be full of charming old men with handlebar moustaches falling off benches, a light, sweet film with serious undertones. I wanted to make a hard-hitting, angry film about what New Labour are doing to this country, and there's a degree of hypocrisy here as I also made a ten-minute portrait of Tony Blair for a party political broadcast in 1997. At the end of one three-hour screening Channel Four's Peter Dale said: "But I wanted a Molly Dineen film," and I said, "But I am Molly Dineen, and I want this film to be more serious, more political, more journalistic." There's the dilemma; trying to make something serious without losing the charm, the slightly offbeat eccentricity expected of the characters in my films.

I disagree when people describe my documentaries as "fly on the wall." They are anything but. I'm eyeing my subjects through a huge movie camera, they're talking to the lens as I'm filming them, and the process is very visible. It's the same with the commentary. I don't want me as a character—there was far too much of me in *Geri*. And I was so damned bossy. You could hear me behind the camera, saying endlessly, "But why don't you just go and see somebody and take a positive approach?" and her in front of the camera, sobbing away in a field. The film is a dialogue between Geri and me, but it shouldn't have been. Normally I'd use me as a springboard, and that's quite nice if the relationship works, because it involves the viewer. If someone looks into the lens and says, "Christ, I'm bored…" they're saying it to the viewer. This was all about what I, Molly, was thinking and saying to her. I couldn't observe properly because I was part of it, but I was also a crew of one. Why don't I use a cameraman? I couldn't bear the frustration of

trying to explain what I want. I look at things and think, "God, that's a good shot or conversation…" and that's where I automatically turn. But not having a sound recordist makes for terribly undisciplined filmmaking.

The sound recordist is your co-pilot on a shoot, and Sarah Jeans worked with me during the shooting of all my films up until *The Ark*. I worked alone on *The Lords' Tale*, the Blair political, and *Geri,* and apart from the fact that it's ludicrous panning the mike with my left hand and trying to shoot with my right, I'd really liked to have had her with me on *Geri*. I found it socially heavy; Geri was quite intense and really needed someone to hang out with while I got on with the shoot. Sarah and I met at film school and she has got this extraordinary way with people. While I was shooting, doing interviews, and directing, she was brilliant at maintaining the atmosphere as well as being an excellent sound recordist. When Colonel Hook came back to England Sarah and I moved in with him for a while, and we cooked, and shopped, and talked together, and it helped create the reality we were trying to capture.

Once I've entered the world of the participants in my films they usually become a part of my life. This sounds as if I use other people's lives for my playtime. It's not that, it's just that I find it really difficult to cut off, go home, have dinner, and then head back the next morning. So, for example, Sarah and I lived in the army barracks in Northern Ireland on and off for a year. On *The Ark*, I spent all day in the zoo and out with the keepers in the evenings. I'd go to the zoo's club for drinks and then hang out in the lodge, where some of the keepers live, and would probably get home around 10 or 11 every night. Obviously, now that I'm married with three children, I can't do that anymore. I felt incredibly frustrated at

Station foreman and London
Underground staff
*Heart of the Angel*, 1989

The Acts of Parliament vault
*The Lords' Tale*, 2002

The Lords' question time
*The Lords' Tale*, 2002

the degree to which I had to treat the making of *The Lords' Tale* like a job, when I knew amazing things were happening at 2am after the House had risen, and someone was hacked off and had too much to drink. I wanted to be there, because next morning I'd almost certainly get a fantastic piece.

I was born into the age of video but have more experience of film, which I prefer. I feel so easy with an Aäton. I love the design of the camera, I love the balance, the weight, and I even like the hold-ups while changing magazines. In that way, I limit the amount of sync conversation because I think in 400 feet at a time. A sad way of putting it, but it's true. With video, the public's relationship to the camera has changed. I command no authority with a little video camera, whereas I do with a film camera. It looks proper, and the public can't use it. I remember on *The Ark* when David Jones, the chief executive, was being kicked out of the zoo, there was this incredible moment of him leaving his office for the last time just as I had my hands in the changing bag loading a magazine. Actually, it was the best thing that could have happened. I was struggling away in the bag instead of staring at him, pointing the camera at him. It totally defused the tension of that moment, and I was able to carry on shooting.

The downside of using film is weight. On *In the Company of Men*, the soldiers wouldn't carry my rucksack on patrols, they had their own, and I found it exhausting tramping around with all my heavy kit. If you work with tape, you can stick the result in your handbag, but you're not coming from anywhere proper, you might as well be a Japanese tourist. Certainly, with the House of Lords, they would have respected me a lot more if I'd had a more serious-looking camera. I think the Lords felt threatened by my being a woman with a little camera, but at the same time they didn't want any intrusion and thanked me for working alone. However, you can't hear half the rushes because there's no sound recordist. This made me sloppier. I can't say it enabled me to shoot more—I always shoot too much: 110 hours of film for *The Ark*, 80 hours for *In the Company of Men,* and acres for *Geri*.

Tape is so ill-disciplined—you shoot carpets, ceilings, the lot. I just keep running; if I turned off and on with the run-up I'd lose it. I could bang on for hours about why I don't like video and hate editing on Avid. It should be magnificent—slinging stuff about and doing a million different cuts—but for me it isn't because it's all open-ended, all up for grabs. I need the closure of cutting film. Maybe because I'm

computer-illiterate I feel removed from my rushes. My editor, a film man, is probably lousy on computers, too, but he's made himself Avid-literate so he can cut documentaries. We forever struggle to describe a shot in order to log it, decide what bin to put the clip in… and how do you describe that?

I've always been excited about the huge stage of television, and I feel angry that it has been degraded and debased. There is no analysis anymore, no editorial line, an absence of professionalism. Everybody films, everyone's on television, the whole thing is blurred. I have no idea where I fit into all this, and sometimes suspect, depressingly, that my films have achieved very little. I had hoped, with the House of Lords film, that I'd really give the government a kick up the arse, but I doubt if they felt kicked. The film does override stereotypes, though. It gets at the real characters of the people involved, which is why I work alone, talking to people, getting to know them—it's how I bring out a character. What I love is confronting an audience with a stereotype, showing it to be false, making them question their prejudices and maybe getting to like the character.

Actually, I was thinking the other day that it's a great privilege to be given a soapbox to rant from.

Lady Margaret Thatcher
(former Prime Minister)
*The Lords' Tale*, 2002

# Alastair Fothergill

**03**

### An introduction

Educated in zoology, schooled in television; one of a small breed of specialists whose love of nature and the animal kingdom finds its way to the screen in the form of documentaries. Fothergill entered the BBC's famous Natural History Unit on graduating from university, and remains there now. Once deskbound, running the department, his enthusiasm for field work has since taken him around the globe producing award-winning wildlife programs. Now he is re-working his outstanding series *The Blue Planet* for theater release, and at the same time developing a major new series with a working title of *Planet Earth* for transmission in 2006.

# Alastair Fothergill

*Bristol, April 15 2002*

I'm a muddy-boot biologist and graduated in zoology in 1983. I got my first job here in the BBC's Natural History Unit. I've been here ever since. My father was a schoolmaster at Harrow School in North London, where I was at school. Our family home was on the north Norfolk coast—a wonderful wild place, fantastic wildlife. That's where I got my passion for the natural world. We humans are much closer to it than we think, and I love to communicate that in films.

To make good wildlife films and get the camera in a position to film the behavior that everybody wants to see, you have to understand animals. That's why we "grow people." We start them on children's programs and short films. They begin as researchers, become assistant producers, then producers. There's really no better way than learning on the job. Television is a technical business, but to be honest, the technical side changes so quickly. I think the thing we need to know, more than anything else, is the skill of storytelling. There are 300 people working here in Bristol, home to the Natural History Unit, producing the largest number of wildlife television, radio, and online pages in the world; we're almost unique and we're 45 years old.

The greatest mentor for me, and I think for most of us, is David Attenborough. I was fortunate to work with him on *The Trials of Life*, a big series on animal behavior in the late '80s and early '90s. He also presented my first series as a producer, *Life in*

*the Freezer*, on Antarctica, and he narrated my *The Blue Planet* series. Apart from being an amazing communicator, David was the greatest director-general the BBC never had. As the controller of BBC2 he commissioned *Civilization* and *Ascent of Man*, and he introduced both color and snooker to BBC Television. I've learnt an awful lot from David Attenborough.

The specialist cameramen we work with spend their whole careers in the wild, and they have been fantastic mentors in many ways, too. I mean, they taught me about patience, and how not to give in with animals. You don't have the same relationship with cameramen as people in the movies or other documentary areas because our cameramen are all specialists. For instance, there are two or three in the world that are brilliant with long lenses; they can follow (in close-up) birds of prey in flight. There are others who are wonderful underwater cameramen and would be useless with a long lens; others who specialize in filming tiny insects. One of the collaborators I regularly work with is the composer George Fenton. George did the music for *The Trials of Life*, *Life in the Freezer*, and most recently *Blue Planet*. He has also composed film music for an enormous slew of successful Hollywood films.

One of the most important aspects about wildlife filmmaking is risk management. You decide to go out to film an animal. It can cost a lot of money. Are you likely to get the behavior you want? You could argue that wildlife films are totally unpredictable in

Alastair Fothergill (left) and crew with Sir David Attenborough, Antarctica *Life in the Freezer*, 1992–93

Alastair Fothergill (left), Paul Atkins, and
Sir David Attenborough, Antarctica
*Life in the Freezer*, 1992–93

Cameraman Doug Allan under the ice
in Greenland
*The Blue Planet*, 1998–2001

Cameraman Peter Scoones and Bluefin
tuna, Japan
*The Blue Planet*, 1998–2001

the sense that in the end, whatever plans you have, nature will always decide what's going to happen. You cannot tell an elephant to come in camera left. I believe successful wildlife films are made by being very organized. I storyboard them in the way you would a drama. And in the cutting room I pass the storyboard onto the editor. In *Blue Planet* we went to far eastern Russia to film the world's largest eagle, a Steller's sea eagle, attacking kittiwakes. This had never been filmed properly before; the eagle had very unpredictable behavior. In the field, the cameraman Simon King and I drew a storyboard. We were there for six weeks. We looked at the behavior, and I explained what the previous sequence was and the sequence we were going to do. For three weeks the eagles didn't take a kill. We changed the storyboard all the time. Literally everyday we redrew it or threw bits out that we had shot. When a film's going to be shot in 30 or 40 locations around the world you need a visual narrative.

Another side of risk management is budgeting. It is difficult, but most film budgets consist of a lot of things that you can work out, like post-production and staffing costs. You can work out two-thirds of it, and the thing we're always driving for is time in the field. A film takes eight or ten weeks to edit; you can't do much about that. We know how many people we need to make a big series. So when we're driving up the budgets or trying to get money out of the market, it's always based on how many days we can put guys in the field. For every sequence that I did for *Blue Planet,* and there were many that we thought were going to be impossible, the first thing was to analyze the risk in relation to the prize. There was one sequence of a pod of Killer whales running down a Gray whale and its calf. We were unbelievably lucky to get that sequence. We spent two seasons achieving it. The scientist we were working with had worked on it for 14 years and had only seen it twice. Probably you shouldn't go for that, because the likelihood is you'd fail. A lot of the sequences for *Blue Planet* did fail. But this was worth the risk. It ended up being a very dramatic seven minutes in the first program that everybody talks about. If you played safe in wildlife films everyone would film the same thing, and if you take too much risk you end up with blank screens, and we very nearly did. It's tricky! When *Life on Earth* went out in 1979, everybody was excited because they got an amazing lion hunt from three camera angles—now it's commonplace. We often have shooting ratios of 20 or 30:1, particularly when filming with high-speed cameras that run 500 frames per second. Actually, with the sort of big series we work on, with difficult logistics, film stock is one of the smallest items of the budget. And if you storyboard you can save on stock and time in the edit. One of the nice things about Bristol is that we have a cottage industry within a mile of this building where a lot of the BBC's post-production work is done. I like to give the editor a very clear vision at the beginning, and then I leave them to it.

Wildlife filmmaking is one of the few areas that still shoot on film. There are three things that keep us on film—first, film cameras are robust and do not suffer from humidity or cold, which video cameras do; second is high-speed cameras. A lot of wildlife photography involves slowing down the action, and although video is just beginning to provide some

Sequence of Killer whales attacking, then injuring Gray whale mother and calf, Monterey, California, *The Blue Planet*, 1998–2001

sort of slow motion, it doesn't match film; and third, the look. Ask people why they like wildlife films, and the first thing they say is the photography. We try to produce visually satisfying products, and video hasn't quite delivered yet. That said, video has provided some fantastic breakthroughs for us. We find video works better underwater. For *Blue Planet*, being able to film in murky conditions was important. Also, video is very good in lowlight—infrared and high-sensitivity conditions. At night we use a lot of video. And, of course, video cameras can be left running for long periods of time just to wait for a bit of behavior, almost like surveillance filming—you can't do that with a 400-foot roll of film.

Many of the things that we film look fantastic on a cinema screen—they're very dramatic, big images. It is a constant frustration that we work on small television screens. I make theatrical-style documentaries. *Blue Planet* did the business in the UK and the US because of style. My films are emotional, and that's to do with the length of sequences and using a Hollywood composer like George Fenton. In fact, [at time of writing] I am

presently in the cutting room turning *Blue Planet* into a movie. I think there could be a real market, certainly in Europe, for theatrical releases of natural history films. The screen size doesn't affect the way we make them. We did a *Blue Planet* concert in London's Royal Festival Hall with an orchestra playing live with a projection on a massive cinema screen. It was a total wow! A very different experience to that of television, so I think we are moviemakers who are forced to put our product out on the small screen.

A lot of our work is "blue chip" natural history. Some in the documentary world never quite take natural history seriously. But wildlife films are documentaries, no question about it. We are about factual accuracy. Even though there may be only one scientist in the world who knows about a particular animal, we make sure that he or she is consulted. We are very proud of that because we want to appeal to, and be respected by, the scientific community. When I was at university, learning about evolution, I was shown *Life on Earth*, and I know that now *Blue Planet* is being used in

pretty well every marine biology course in the country. That said, we are still storytellers. Of course, documentary filmmakers have their boundaries and we have ours. There are obviously a number of ethical questions to grapple with. One is telling the truth about the environment—the *Blue Planet* series consisted of eight beautiful films about the oceans, but very little about the environment. We, in the unit, get to see a lot of the damage that's being done to our planet. Another is about third-world cultures—we meet people all over the world, and how we portray them is an important issue for us. Then anthropomorphism—the extent to which we become anthropomorphic about animals. And bringing predation and sex into people's living rooms is a delicate issue—we are guests in their homes. We could say, "You're free to switch it off," but I don't think that's good enough. We have to recognize that at eight in the evening many families are having dinner, so do they want to see wildebeest being ripped apart? Yes, we've got to be true to nature, but it's how we do it, the context it is put in. If you see the lion cubs starving then you understand why the lion kills the wildebeest, in fact

Interview
Alastair Fothergill

Steller's sea eagle, Kamchatka, Russia

Storyboard for Steller's sea
eagle sequence
*The Blue Planet*, 1998–2001

CU Kittiwake flying/dodging (may need flap)

CU Eagle approach

Several wider shots of eagles prospecting cliffs and kittiwakes reacting as material allows.

MCU Eagle attempted strike

Kittiwake kill.

If Eagle taking bird from sea O.K. or improvement on kittiwake, then use shots of birds on water (guillimots)

Kittiwakes return to cliff

you're delighted that she's succeeded. But you can tell a lot without actually showing it. So we don't dwell on blood and guts.

We are very aware of "the animal Top Ten"—the charismatic animals, the lions, orangutans, dolphins. But what really fascinates me is that we can create charisma. I remember a BBC executive saying about David Attenborough's *The Private Life of Plants*, "How are you going to make a film on leaves interesting?" Yet through computerized time-lapse, the plants were given charismatic qualities. There was a sequence of the growth of the common blackberry bramble, which became horrifically triffid-like by speeding up its movements.

Because this is an unpredictable medium, I try and make it as predictable as I can. Firstly by being clear about the message of the film. Then the structure and how the programs work together. And the duration is vital. I don't write long scripts because it is a waste of time. I want to know the storyline; I want to know about the emotions and the mood. Then a storyboard of every sequence. That piece of paper stays with me through every waking hour.

I think about it, review it, and, if I get a sequence that goes well, I might extend it.

The opening three minutes of *Blue Planet* probably cost more than any single wildlife sequence I've ever filmed. I wanted to film the blue whale feeding in the open ocean. First, I needed a Cessna aircraft to locate the whales, then a very expensive boat and two or three cameramen. About 90 percent of the shots are absolutely useless. In *Blue Planet* we had sequences that cost £50–£60,000, but also had sequences that cost £3–£4,000. I wanted the sequence because the blue whale is the largest animal on the planet, but we don't know where it goes to breed—a symbol of our ignorance. So if you have a very expensive three minutes you need a cheap five minutes. You know if it's in Britain, not using a boat, filming a robin, you could get a decent three-minute sequence in a couple of days.

All filmmaking, certainly wildlife filmmaking, needs light and shade and change of pace. If it's endless action, action, action, the viewer gets blown away. There is a generation growing up now that is used to very dynamic visual media. We have programs like

*Wildlife Battlefields* and *Weird Nature* that are visually extraordinary. But there is a place for a slow, lyrical, beautiful wildlife documentary, and there's a place for natural history MTV. The BBC is a canvas for high-quality programs.

There are two sides to my job—getting the pictures, and knowing how to structure the pictures to tell the stories. With the first there are three simple rules which I've learnt—first, you won't get pictures sitting in your tent; second, you can only be in one place at a time; and third, it's only television. By that I mean, nature will screw you up, so just be patient, think about the audience, and remember they don't necessarily have the passion that you have. An example: *Blue Planet*, eight hours on fish, with extraordinarily detailed biological stories, which some people like and some don't. But I wanted to catch the emotion of the storm and the seas. And *Blue Planet* got 13 million viewers. After the soap operas like *EastEnders* and *Coronation Street*, it was the most watched program on British television.

Camp on location during filming, Antarctica
*The Blue Planet*, 1998–2001

Inuit guides leading crew on skidoos
*The Blue Planet*, 1998–2001

Cameraman Doug Allan filming in an ice hole, Arctic Bay, Nunavut, Canada
*The Blue Planet*, 1998–2001

Beluga whales surfacing in front of
Doug Allan, Canadian arctic
*The Blue Planet*, 1998–2001

# Hans-Dieter Grabe

04

### An introduction

He came in from the cold and for 40 years produced a library of work for Germany's second television channel ZDF. Hans-Dieter Grabe's acute awareness and sensitivity gave rise to a batch of documentaries examining the conscience of Germany. Forever an individualist, his strain of program-making has kept him at the forefront. Whether on the streets of post-war Berlin or war-torn Vietnam, with victims of the Holocaust or the street-children of Rwanda; his films are quiet but penetrating studies of the people he identifies with, and for whom he so obviously feels affection.

# Hans-Dieter Grabe

*Mainz, January 10, 2003*

The first significant event in my life was the destruction of my hometown of Dresden by allied bombing in February 1945. This had such a strong and lasting impact on me because, until then, Dresden had hardly been touched by bombing. On one night, the war began for me. Previously it had only existed on the radio, when I heard that squadrons of bombers were flying over the Ruhr on the way to Berlin. Now the reality hit me.

Two weeks before the end of the war, our house was bombed, so at the end of 1945 we moved to Cottbus to live with an aunt. It was a painful move, because I loved Dresden. I'd been to Cottbus before, to visit my aunt, and during the journey, a fellow traveler in the train asked where we were going, and my mother said "Cottbus," to which he said, "Oh God, that's the arsehole of Europe." Before we moved I spent the summer in Dresden— it was a time of liberation for me. I was an only child and now I came into contact with many children whom I'd never seen before. Fences were down between the houses, and also between people. We played in the ruins, went into gardens and stole apples, cherries, and pears. And when the water and gas pipes were being repaired, deep trenches were dug in the streets and we could play wonderful games in them. It was a very creative time for me. And so then, to be torn from the city because of the destruction of our home, was terrible.

I had been born into a middle-class family in 1937. My father was a colonel in the *Luftwaffe* (Air Force), although not a Nazi Party member. After the war my father ran into problems with the Russian authorities and they took him prisoner. He disappeared for many weeks. It was impossible to find out where he was being held—not unusual in those days. He had a heart complaint and so he was returned to us. Looking back, I cannot blame the Russians for taking him away. He'd been a member, no matter how innocent, of the army that committed monstrous crimes, especially in Russia. That an

officer was not a Nazi was not unusual, but what was highly unusual was that my father stayed in the then-Eastern Zone. Smart people preferred to go to the Western Zones. The fact that he stayed was due to political naïvety. My father was a forthright, straightforward person who'd never take a short-cut to advantage himself. He was an opponent of the communist state, whose political thinking was absolutely foreign to him. I think I have taken a straightforwardness and simplicity from him. I believe there were two attempts to persuade him to work for the *Stasi* (the East German secret police), because, through his work as a door-to-door insurance agent, he came into contact with so many people. Undoubtedly, things would have been easier for a few years as far as our standard of living was concerned, but he never even considered it.

I completed secondary education in Cottbus and then faced the question of what to do? I wanted to study, but the choice of subjects was not exactly simple in a state like the German Democratic Republic (GDR). I would not choose a subject which led in a political direction that I was not prepared to follow. Moreover, as a child of middle-class parents, I didn't know whether I would even be allowed to go to university. Then I read that the German Academy for Film Studies had opened in Potsdam-Babelsberg. I had always loved film, but never considered it a possible profession. After several tests, with enormous luck I was selected as a student of directing, and started in 1955. Of course, would-be film directors were expected to join the Party, but I didn't. One could get a great career as a director of feature films, but making documentaries was far more politically complex. Documentary films don't get made without some commitment to reality, whereas features could be forced to represent Utopia. And that was where the friction lay for me. In our first films at the Academy, when we turned the camera on normal life, disputes began with members of the academic authorities. It was the question of where to shoot: in areas of

Samuel, one of Kigali's street children, Rwanda
*These Pictures Haunt Me—Alfred Jahn, M.D.*,
2002

27-year-old Do Sanh, Ho-Chi-Minh City
*Do Sanh—The Last Film*, 1998

new development or old streets with beautiful but rundown houses; a new state-run supermarket or a street-market; in a railway station half-dilapidated by the war or a new station? To shoot people with care-worn faces and old clothes or well-nourished people with smart suits? We students realized that by making documentaries you could draw attention to your product, and often, we wanted to be provocative. We wanted people to talk and argue about our work. We saw how easy it was to irritate our lecturers or Party functionaries, merely by placing a camera in the center of life. There were 12 of us in our directing group, and including myself, just two wanted to make documentaries.

Mentally many people in the GDR were always sitting on a packed suitcase. The question was, did we want to live in the GDR or not? There was never a simple answer as the policies of the Party kept changing, and because the borders with Berlin were still open, we knew that, if we had to, we could leave. But in 1959 it was obvious to those living around Berlin that there would be some kind of restriction on access to the West. My wish, after leaving university, was to work in a studio making documentaries. I learnt of a position at the film studio, but it was to be given only to a Party member. So I knew I would have to work in television, and I knew that would lead to huge problems. Six months before completing my course, I decided to leave the GDR. I left with a heavy heart—I'd really enjoyed the Academy, I had no contacts in the West, and I didn't even know if I'd find work, nor if I'd ever be able to return. I arrived in West Berlin, and with the only five West-Deutschmarks I had, I bought a directory of film companies. Suddenly I was full of optimism; there were so many. I hitched through West Germany—Hamburg, Frankfurt, Stuttgart, and Munich, but many companies were no longer in existence, or

were father-and-son outfits that couldn't use anyone, or they made advertising or sex films—they laughed at me. There had been a kind of film academy in Munich, where the library still existed. The librarian gave me a little work to earn some money. She also knew the Director of Bavarian Television and arranged an appointment with him. He passed me to the light entertainment department, whose chief had bought a stack of films from the Prix Italia. German versions had to be made. So I stayed in a worker's hostel and while others slept, I translated scripts. As the cutting rooms were only free at night, I worked there nights, cutting and pasting the films using film cement. I was so happy! I had left the GDR in late November 1959 and by January 1960 I had a job.

The possibility arose to work in current affairs and regional programing, and I worked in Munich for just under three years. Admittedly, I couldn't do exactly what I had in mind for myself, but it was an important experience. I got to know life in this new, and for me strange, society. I traveled with the crews, did research, and was in touch with politicians and company directors. This was all an important preparation for my real documentary work, which I took up at Zweites Deutsches Fernsehen (ZDF, Germany's second national television network). Here I was to realize projects I'd had in mind as a student; films about Hiroshima and Nagasaki, about concentration camps, their victims, and the resistance movement. The victims of the atomic bombs had concerned me since childhood, as in early 1945 I experienced the entire city of Dresden being destroyed, causing about 40,000 deaths. It struck me how 2,500 planes were needed to drop their bombs. Only a few weeks later, on 6 August, I learnt that a single plane with a single bomb was enough to kill about 85,000 Japanese on one day, and 130,000 further during the following

days, weeks, months, and years. This knowledge was embedded in me from early childhood. So it was not unnatural for me to follow a career which allowed me to make films that could contribute to peace and be against war. This may sound clichéd, but for a long time I labored under the illusion that film could change society. I now know this isn't so.

My first really personal film for ZDF was in 1966—*Hope, Five Times a Day*—a portrait of a railway station on the border between East and West, at which five trains stopped each day. Documentaries in those days were basically journalistic projects, with a lot of research packed in to impress the viewer. *Hope, Five Times a Day* was very different. The ZDF editorial staff had absolutely no interest in this portrait of a small town and its station. I was often confronted with this attitude, because my films concentrated on one particular point, and person. *The Women Who Cleared Away the Ruins of Berlin* was made in 1967, and focused on the tremendous hard work of the women cleaning the post-war rubble in the cities. This was my first film where I spoke in detail with people on camera, and that wasn't normal for the times. These women were important witnesses of an era, but television did not consider such people to be witnesses; only VIPs, politicians, officers, churchmen. Not these ordinary people who spoke about their work, what they had to eat, and the illnesses they had to cope with. There were hardly any machines and hardly any men; they were either dead or in prison camps somewhere. It was also important that the film dealt with peace—this was the time of the Cold War. In documentaries from East Germany there was a lot of talk of peace—clichés for the most part. Some colleagues in my company criticized my film, saying it could set people in the West thinking that it came from "over there." The film is still shown on television and has lost none of its liveliness. At ZDF,

I could do the things I'd always wanted to do and not have to worry about paying the rent because some superior didn't agree with my ideas. I had the time to work on the things which were important to me. I regarded my position as employee not just as a "chance" to work in this way, but an "obligation." I kept this up for 40 years. My films became increasingly political and there was sometimes a certain amount of resistance to them, and mistrust, because my topics and methods were unusual.

In 1970, I was in Vietnam. Early in the Vietnam War the Americans wanted Germany to join them. Fortunately, the German government refused. But they didn't want the USA to stand alone in their fight against Communism, so a hospital ship was sent to Vietnam. There alongside US warships in Saigon lay the German hospital ship, Helgoland, flying the German ensign. When I first went to Vietnam, I hoped to make a film about civilian victims of the war on that ship, but in 1966 there were none in Saigon. Four years later, I returned to the Helgoland, now birthed at Da Nang, in the center of the war, where we shot *Only Light Skirmishes in the Da Nang Area*. There were few newspaper headlines in Germany about the war; the film's title is taken from one of them. Our film showed exactly what these "light skirmishes" meant, how these ruined civilians came onto the ship as if on a conveyor belt. Our film was sure to attract attention and sympathy back in Germany, and it did make a deep impression with the press and on the viewers. Until then, there hadn't been a film which so radically portrayed the consequences of war. My cameraman, Carl Franz Hutterer, more than any other cameraman, was capable of working with a hand-held camera and no additional artificial light—a prerequisite to working in the wards of the hospital ship. Before we set off for Vietnam we discussed in detail our expectations and how to go about shooting, so when the camera was running I never had to say a word. We agreed to document absolutely faithfully the work of the medical staff. Hutterer had to work intuitively, because obviously I couldn't say, "We'll do that scene again." Unfortunately, the film has remained valid to this day. The showing of wounds in close-up was not normal then, but we had to show the

devastation of the body in precise detail—we owed it to those broken people. They offered their bodies for us to film so we felt this was a way to contribute to the ending of the war. Arguably the Vietnam War was brought to an end by films such as this. Even now it's difficult for me to watch the film. During the shooting we considered the effect the images would have on those in charge at ZDF. Perhaps the thought of censorship drove us. A film can generate its own strength, and in fact no one at ZDF dared propose any changes. The film has been constantly repeated both on ZDF and the 3-Sat station. When the Berlin Wall came down and the world changed in 1989, I thought there would be no more wars and films like this would no longer be necessary. It turned out to be the opposite!

*20 Miles to Saigon* was the first significant film I made that featured one person in particular: Roger Leonard. I met Roger by chance outside Saigon with his three Vietnamese wives. The text in the film was only in the form of captions. Even in *Only Light Skirmishes in the Da Nang Area* the text had been sparse. Sometimes it is important to stand forward as the author, and sometimes it's an intrusion. I have made a film with text only on stills, where the moving picture stopped and spoken text is heard over the stills. The nature of the film dictated this approach for me—it was about suicide, and I preferred not to superimpose text over people.

*Mendel Szajnfeld's Second Journey to Germany* was conceived as quite a different film from its final version. I had been considering the subject of long-term damage—cases of concentration camp inmates, people who had been tortured. I met Mendel in Norway—a former prisoner in German camps in Poland during the Second World War, whose mental and physical health was in a very poor state. He worked in a metal processing plant and long-term damage had made him deteriorate to the point of his hardly being able to work. He talked about the causes of his suffering in German labor camps so expressively and so well in German that I decided to concentrate the film on him. I had taken the risk of reducing a wide-ranging subject, that of long-term damage, and my approach

worked. Bare facts don't move anyone, but facts about a person can. After the war Mendel had spent two years in a camp in Bavaria, and he was now fighting for an increase in his injury pension, which he received from Munich. I had the idea of filming him on a train from Oslo to Munich. I proposed to accompany him and pay his travel expenses so we could talk about his life and his illness, during the journey. Mendel was suffering headaches, nightmares, and had kidney and heart problems, but his doctor agreed to allow this sick man to go with us. Like many who had been in camps, Mendel hoped his involvement in the film would contribute to preventing such things happening again. Here we were traveling to the very country in which all those terrible things had happened to him, where many of his relatives had been murdered, and he was making this trip with a group of Germans. This put him under pressure, but luckily not adversely so. His testimony had an unbelievable strength—exactly what I had been hoping for. Later, I went to Oslo to show him the finished film. His doctor, Professor Eittinger, held his hand throughout. After the television broadcast there were a lot of newspaper reviews praising both the film and Mendel. He received lots of mail from Germany and relationships developed as a result.

Twenty-eight years later I went to Oslo to see Mendel. Perhaps as a consequence of his experience with the film, he had written a book about his life. This was the man who, before he met us, had never spoken about his life with anyone except his psychiatrist. As a Jew he felt useless, because Jews were not given the opportunity to contribute. He spoke of his work in the Nazi labor camps and the pride he took, even there, not to please his masters, but to maintain his own worth. He proved he could be useful, and not cave in at the first blow—a kind of resistance and victory. He tried to prove to himself and to others that, as a Jew, as an apparent inferior, no one could break his spirit with hunger and blows. Sitting in an Oslo café, his eyes shone with life as he told me of accompanying groups of travelers, many of them school children, to the former German concentration camps in Poland, and acting as a witness to what happened

Hans-Dieter Grabe (left) interviewing Do
Sanh in 1974, Datat, South Vietnam
*Do Sanh*, 1991

there. He felt he could still be of use to other people. I then had the idea of a second film: *Mendel is Alive*, a man alive who ought to be dead. That, alone, is wonderful. He so enjoyed his coffee and eating with me, when he cut bread it was like a sacred act. Although not directly comparable, I was reminded of my past and the hunger after the war; I felt close to him. I shot this second film alone. It's a great thing when shooting a documentary, to be able to take one's time, and not to worry about colleagues whose bellies rumble at one o'clock. I had worried that shooting by myself wouldn't work if my face was hidden behind the camera during interviews. I believed my facial reactions were important for the interviewee, the way I showed my curiosity to gain maximum response. Although I wouldn't repeat the experience in every case, there are times when it works, but the conversation should not be involved, and never polemic. Prior knowledge of the person is needed, and in Mendel's case I knew, from the first film, that he didn't need my face in order to talk. Often he would stare out of the window or right past it, giving the impression I was sitting next to the camera, not behind it.

I was a one-off at ZDF. There was no provision made for a job such as mine, working as a permanent member of staff. Actually there were also no official slots for my long films. And although I could only work with the support of a lot of important people in the company, nevertheless there were always problems. Now I am surrounded by colleagues doing entirely different work, who perhaps are not always inclined to show sympathy for my problems or wishes. For example, colleagues work mainly on topical programs which are quick to make. The costs of my programs were quite modest, but it's not enough to save money in shooting and then need 50 days for editing. Those 50 days for example will continue to be a problem for the heads of production. Years ago I was surrounded by colleagues who knew my work and way of working. Nowadays, if I said to my head of production, "I need the same time to shoot as I had for the last film," probably he wouldn't understand what I was talking about. I can no longer justify the necessity of my work on the experience of earlier films, because no one has time to look at what we made previously. Anyway, if I were to make another film I would also need the strength, not just the ability, of a cameraman. On the recent shoot in Rwanda, I felt I was reaching my physical limits—something I had not foreseen.

If young people want to make documentaries they will no longer be able to do so inside the television companies. Their paths lie outside. I don't want to put down the work done in the broadcast companies nowadays; I believe that working in such companies is extraordinarily important, satisfying, and exciting, especially for young people. But the possibility of producing documentaries as a regular member of staff has become the exception. So documentary filmmakers have to work with independent companies or use their abilities as independent producers to try to get films made in cooperation with the editorial staff of television companies.

Top left: Mendel Szajnfeld interviewed by Hans-Dieter Grabe (right). Lower left: Mendel Szajnfeld taking psychiatric tests, Oslo. Center: Mendel Szajnfeld
*Mendel Szajnfeld's Second Journey to Germany*, 1971

Left: Mendel Szajnfeld at home, Oslo
*Mendel is Alive*, 1999

# Patricio Guzmán

**05**

## An introduction

If there are elder statesmen among documentary makers, surely Patricio Guzmán is one. Born a Chilean, he studied film in Franco's Spain before returning to record Salvador Allende's revolution. Guzmán became a chronicler of the great experiment and subsequently the disastrous backlash of the Chilean right-wing under the leadership of the infamous General Pinochet. Unlike other documentary makers, who must turn to the archives to reconstruct history, Guzmán shot the actual raw material, a witness to history as it was happening, and used his own footage to produce crucial and exhaustive works such as *The Battle of Chile* and *The Pinochet Case*.

# Patricio Guzmán

*Paris, September 9 and 15, 2002*

It rains a lot in Chile, and is often very cold. I was four when my father left, and so I lived with my mother in Viña del Mar, a wonderful little town on the coast. I wasn't a very good student and passed through school with no idea at all of what I would do as an adult. I didn't feel very comfortable at university either. I tried theater studies, then history, finally philosophy, and didn't finish any of them. But together with two friends, one studying philosophy and the other theater, I directed eight short films using an 8mm camera—some fiction, some animation, probably influenced by Norman McLaren, the Scottish-born filmmaker who painted directly onto celluloid, and worked for a while with John Grierson. Twice a week I went to the cinema and saw nearly every North American picture of the '40s and '50s. At this time, there were few Chilean filmmakers. I left university mainly for economic reasons, and found work as a copywriter in an advertising agency. At the end of the '50s documentaries were beginning to be taken seriously. I saw films by Jacques-Yves Cousteau, Louis Malle, and Walt Disney. I didn't like fiction and was more interested in making animated drawings and shooting stop-frame animation. This, for me, was a way to talk about our history. There were two movements which had a profound influence on me: Free Cinema and New Wave, both of which are near to documentary. These kind of films arrived in Chile around 1961 to 1962.

I wanted to get copies made of our 8mm films, so I asked the Cinematographic Institute for its help. The head of the department liked the films and invited me to become a student at the school. I went each morning and continued at the advertising agency in the afternoons and evenings. After three years I decided to go to Spain to the Madrid Cinema School. At the same time a cinematographic movement was emerging in Chile—very political, very creative, and very Latin American. There was a meeting in Viña del Mar of Latin American filmmakers which marked the beginning of the new Latin American cinema. But it was in Madrid where I quickly became politically minded and began to learn about Latin America and its colonization by European imperialism, and the evil of economic dependence. I discovered J. Edgar Hoover and Che Guevara. When Salvador Allende became President, I went straight back to Chile.

He had been campaigning for 18 years, having started in 1952. Allende was already the leader of the Socialist Party when I was a little boy, but I felt no particular sympathy for him. At that age I did not understand exactly what he wanted to do, and I tended more to the political center—Christian Democracy. My political way of thinking had awakened while I had been in Franco's Spain, and at the university in Madrid there was a strong political consciousness on the part of the students.

*The Battle of Chile*, 1973–79

President Salvador Allende
*The Battle of Chile*, 1973–79

Interview
Patricio Guzmán

Above: Patricio Guzmán (second from
right) interviewing Judge Juez Guzmán
(second from left). Right: Patricio
Guzmán (left) and crew filming
demonstrators announcing the names
of ex-torturers still in service in the
Chilean government
*The Pinochet Case*, 2000

*Madrid*, 2002

So, Allende becoming president, I felt that I absolutely had to be in Chile. I went without knowing what work I could find. I had been five years in Madrid. As I left the airplane I immediately had the idea of doing a documentary about what was going on. There were streets full of demonstrations, paintings on the walls, Allende's campaign speeches talking about nationalizing steel, coal, electricity, and the banks. The day Allende came to power he started to implement his program of popular unity. Those of us who supported Allende thought it was possible to make a revolution without a civil war, and at first there was no danger from the military.

Together with a cameraman and sound recordist using an Arriflex camera and a Perfect Tone sound recorder without synchronization—terrible!— we shot a film on the streets, all hand-held. A celebration, an epic, a film of pure enthusiasm. Looking back on that period it is incredible to think what the bourgeoisie did—such a great act of injustice. Half the Chilean people destroyed, and yet still the Chilean right wing will not apologize for the assassinations and murders. For me, it is as if the coup d'état took place yesterday.

There is a poetic aspect to reality which I like very much, but never manage to pursue. Whenever I try to make a more poetic film, an historical film emerges. Recently I have begun to do small films about cities, like *Madrid*, which give me great satisfaction. Making *The Pinochet Case* these past three years has been very demanding. And now I'm beginning a film about Allende that will take perhaps another three years.

In May 1972 Chris Marker, the French filmmaker [and ex-journalist, whose original name was Christian François Bouche-Villeneuve], came to Chile with Costa-Gavras to see what was going on, and by chance he saw my film, *The First Year*. Marker contacted me to say he would have liked to make a similar film, but as I had already done so, might he distribute mine in other countries? Marker was enormously generous, as this was my first professional film. In October of that year there was a big strike organized by the political right of Chile. Everything was paralyzed, and I recognized that I had to continue with another film about the revolution, which subsequently became *The Battle of Chile*. But I needed film stock to shoot on and so I wrote to Marker asking if he could help, because the embargo of Chile made it impossible to get hold of raw stock. He managed to send the material and we shot until the day of the coup d'état.

Then I was arrested and taken to the National Stadium in Santiago. Naturally, I was very frightened; they told me I would be executed in the morning. But the following morning we were ordered to board a bus. In the meantime the military were searching my home and removed cans and cans of film. Fortunately none of the cans contained negatives. We were driven to the Chilean Stadium, a terrible place where we had heard they were assassinating people. Quite suddenly they changed their plan and we returned to the National Stadium, where I was placed in isolation. This surely meant I was condemned to die. The next day, they moved me back with the others—all had had similar experiences. I was questioned for two weeks by the military, but they couldn't understand what I was doing. They considered me of no importance. I told them that I was filming for French television. In reality, I had actually hidden everything. After being set free, my Spanish film school colleagues got a collection together, enough for me to leave Chile and fly to Madrid. The material we had shot was smuggled out in the diplomatic bag of the Swedish Embassy. Jorge Müller, the cameraman, stayed in Santiago thinking there was no danger. A year later he was arrested with his girlfriend, the actress Carmen Bueno. It is still not known what happened to them—they disappeared along with so many others.

I experienced a form of censorship with the old GDR (East Germany)—they made cuts in *The Battle of Chile*. And in Chile itself, none of my films has ever been passed for screening in cinemas or presented on television. In Moscow *The Battle of Chile* was screened once, but never again.

Judge Juez Guzmán (right) searching in the north Chilean desert for evidence— bones of Pinochet's "disappeared" *The Pinochet Case*, 2000

Luisa Toledo, one of the victims of Pinochet's dictatorship *The Pinochet Case*, 2000

Interview
Patricio Guzmán

*Obstinate Memory*, 1997

I spend a lot of time debating with myself, and then with the camera operator and the editor, how best to tell the story. So the approach I take with the cameraman is to tell him what I want—we talk a lot about the film beforehand, we make tests, and then I let him improvise. The principal thing is to tell the story in the best way; that's what I'm occupied with. But I am more controlling in my relationship with the editor—I like my films to be very detailed, and I tend to instruct the editor accordingly, although I believe documentaries have a will of their own. There comes a point when they acquire a life, quite by themselves, and suddenly the film is made. Perhaps the secret is to be very free, sincere, honest, and direct. My films are very much a personal statement, although my voice may not actually be heard.

I use commentary only as an aid to understanding. It must be functional, direct, and clear. I like the text to be short and simple. I'd prefer not to use commentary at all, but that's impossible. There are almost no interviews in *The Battle of Chile*, and in *The Pinochet Case* and *Southern Cross*, a history of Latin America from a religious perspective and the

"theology of liberation," interviewees provide a natural commentary. But in *Obstinate Memory*, in which I returned to Santiago to find those who I had featured in *The Battle of Chile* 20 years earlier, there is neither one nor the other, as it is about my life. For me, conducting interviews is one of the most difficult things to accomplish; extracting something new or emotional is very hard—I'm referring to genuine confessions. I undertake to be faithful, to be honest, not to manipulate, nor betray, and normally people respond by giving me the liberty to use what they say without constraint. But it requires a level of mutual confidence, friendship, even affection. There exists an invisible line, beyond which anything is possible—there are no rules, no stereotypes, and no certainties. Of course, I don't believe in objectivity; that's an invented concept which has nothing to do with artistic creativity. Everything I have done I did because I was motivated and passionate about it—but objective, never!

Often one can make a film in several quite different ways. But I tend to go with an emotional stream; there is an energy in people that I try to be sensitive to. In this way there's less danger

of getting lost, but it's a blind way of proceeding— I have to feel my way carefully. In reality there is nothing definitive. I have a metabolism of insecurity. From childhood I had the feeling of never being sure of doing well or not. And it costs me personally to maintain the power invested in me as the director, because I regard power as one of the great dangers in life. And I have to recognize that I'm not capable of confronting power. Perhaps this is at the heart of my documentary work. I never felt confident of finishing anything. I'm now 61 years old and feel the same anxiety I had 25 years ago. Probably a condition always present for the artist. So I say to the young would-be documentary filmmakers, "Make it. Do it. But be conscious of what it means to be a documentary filmmaker—it's a lot of hard work, badly paid, often lacking in recognition, and subjects are frequently very complex. Like jazz, it requires improvisation and risk, sometimes even physical risk. Then there are long periods locked up in the edit. And the only way to deal with all this is to regard the work as a vocation, and with great professionalism."

Patricio Guzmán next to a poster for
*The Battle of Chile*, 1973–79

Patricio Guzmán and participants
*Southern Cross*, 1989–92

Mayan mother and child
*Southern Cross*, 1989–92

# Bonnie Sherr Klein

06

### An introduction

One of a group of women who took on the male-dominated world and turned it on its head. A passionate believer in the rights of women, Klein was one of the core group in the National Film Board of Canada's unique Studio D, where women filmmakers made documentaries about women, for women. Klein's notoriety came with her investigation into the world of pornography, a film whose impact is as significant today as it was some 20 years ago. Klein's motivation and commitment to the cause of women and what she refers to as "the other half" has never faltered.

# Bonnie Sherr Klein

*Vancouver, November 23 and 24, 2002*

Being socially concerned is partly due to my Jewish education, which taught me "Tikkun Olam," —"healing of the world"— and also some of my early experiences with Quakers who held a strong commitment to peace and social justice.

I was born in Philadelphia in 1941, went to public schools, Jewish day high school, then Barnard, a women's college at Columbia University in New York. I did an interdisciplinary major in American Studies. I thought of doing law, but was told it was not a profession for women—and this was a prestigious women's college in 1960! In fact I was mad about theater and went every night I could, and went on to do an MA in theater at Stanford, California. The film department was in the basement of the theater, so I took a minor in film. The one teacher, Henry Breitrose, taught documentary only. I'd never seen a documentary; the first we saw were from the National Film Board of Canada (NFB), brought in by several wonderful Québecois filmmakers.

It was the beginning of the civil rights and anti-nuclear movements. I was always very active in political and social affairs, so seeing these documentaries it struck me how this was an incredible combination of my passion for theater and my need to do some social good. Documentary had powerful social and educational value in one exciting package. The NFB became my Mecca and I switched to major in film. The department was good on structure but poor on production. There were a dozen of us and we crewed on each other's films. My thesis film, *For All My Students*, was about teaching black high-school students. I spent a year raising the money and was finally sponsored by the US Department of Education. The money arrived the week before school was out. We film students had never taken sync-sound and had to hire an Eclair camera, which came up on a bus from Hollywood. We were unpacking it and reading the directions as we went. George Stoney, one of the deans of documentary film in the US, came as a visiting professor. While I edited the film he was my supervisor. He took one look at the rushes and said, "You'll never make a film of this"—that became our standing joke. While at Stanford, George made a

few films about mental health and heart disease. Anyway, I put my film together and George hired me to be his production manager, casting director, and sound engineer—I came cheap. As I knew his material, he asked me if I would come to New York with him to assist his editor. So in 1966 I went. He had a crusty English editor, and I thought I knew much more than her—I'd just graduated film school and I was a pain in the ass. But George was my mentor and still is.

I freelanced in New York and met a guy who was a conscientious objector to the Vietnam War. We were both involved in the anti-war movement. This guy ended up being my husband, Michael. I was invited to show my student film at the Grierson Seminar, and Michael appeared at the seminar with his draft notice. That very day I'd seen Beryl Fox's *The Mills of the Gods* which she made for the Canadian Broadcasting Corporation (CBC)'s fabulous *This Week Has Seven Days*. I didn't really know the difference between CBC and NFB, I didn't know Toronto from Montreal, but here was this film, made by a woman, which showed exactly what was going on in Vietnam. There was nothing of what was happening in Vietnam on American television, and this woman went out in a helicopter (the "Mills") and talked to young guys delightedly shooting Vietcong. It was very, very strong. Anyway, Michael says, "I have a draft notice," and I say, "Well, you have to make a choice between going to jail and going to Canada. If you go to jail, that's your choice. If you go to Canada, I will marry you and go with you."

It was 1967; these were exciting times in Canada. Michael got a job offer and that allowed us to cross the border. I immediately went to the NFB and wandered the corridors knocking on the doors of people whose credits I recognized from seeing their films at Stanford. I ended up in the office of John Kemeny, who hired me to edit and direct in the *Challenge for Change* series, a project designed to use film as a tool for social change across Canada— politicians set programs in motion, and filmmakers recorded the reactions of communities and gave people their say. The films were screened in the Government departments that had commissioned the work in the first place. It was an

Bonnie Sherr Klein teaching in Rochester,
New York, 1972

interesting loop. The program had been running for some time using 16mm film, which was quite clumsy, what with having to send the material back to the lab in Montreal, the expense, and no immediate feedback for the people in the films.

By now it was 1968 or so, and Michael was working as a volunteer doctor in a free medical clinic in a poor area of Montreal called St Jacques—this was before Medicare. A citizens' committee made up primarily of welfare recipients had set up the clinic. I'd never seen such politically astute and involved people. Through Dorothy Hénaut, a writer at the NFB, I became aware of Sony's new half-inch portable videotape recorder. So we thought we could do a project in which we used video instead of film and people could make their own material without our intervention. It was a really interesting experiment. George Stoney had been brought from the US to head the *Challenge for Change* program. Suspicious of video, he told us, "You can only do it if you shoot a 16mm film documenting it." So I had to direct a film while Dorothy and I worked with the St Jacques citizens' committee to help them use video. One of the interesting things was that even though I was a professional filmmaker I didn't know about video at all, so in a sense we were learning together. In fact at the beginning of *VTR St Jacques*, Dorothy's ten-year-old son is seen showing all of us what plug goes where. Working with the committee

was fascinating, as they shot on the streets, and outside hospitals and welfare offices because they weren't allowed to shoot inside—they were kicked out of every place they went. They organized a press conference to introduce the committee and the clinic. The journalists got furious that the citizens' committee were documenting it, and said, "You're not supposed to shoot us, we're supposed to shoot you!" Every night we and the committee looked at the rushes and decided what to edit into a half-hour tape. The original French title was *Operation Boule de Neige*, and the process culminated in "Operation Boule de Neige" (Snowball), a week-long blitz of showing the tape in churches around Montreal's St Jacques neighborhood, where people gathered to see themselves and their neighbors, and to discuss the issues raised, which was also recorded. This was the beginning of community access television. *VTR St Jacques* documents the whole process, and was widely shown throughout the world, especially by George Stoney, who went on to promote community access to cable television in the US.

I also made a film about the St Jacques clinic called *Citizens' Medicine* before going back to the States; Michael, meanwhile, had been re-classified by the US military, so we went to Rochester, New York, for him to do post-doctoral work. I expected everyone to be really excited to have a hotshot NFB director

around. Instead I found myself blacklisted because of a film I made for *Challenge for Change* about Saul Alinsky organizing Rochester's black community against the Eastman Kodak company. So I founded Portable Channel, a video access center, and trained local people, especially women, to make videotapes. The tapes were technically primitive, but amazingly were broadcast on the local public television station on a program we called *Homemade TV*. We stayed in Rochester for five years, but I missed film and Canada, so I decided to return to the NFB, emigrating voluntarily this time.

It was International Year of the Woman, and the NFB had just started a women's film unit, known as Studio D, headed by Kathleen Shannon, to bring the missing perspective of women to film. I had known Kathleen as an editor when I was a director on the *Challenge for Change* film; she became my other mentor. She was absolutely brilliant and totally committed. With a nickels-and-dimes budget, we produced a catalog-full of significant films. It was the only women's film unit of its kind in the world, a collective really, and was government-funded. When I came to the Film Board there were only three women directors in the whole large institution. So Studio D started *Just a Minute*, a project in which 30 women filmmakers around Canada each got to make a one-minute film. It was the beginning for a lot of women who later went on to great film careers.

Far left: St Jacques, Montreal. Left: Young St Jacques residents watching *VTR St Jacques*. Above: Bonnie Sherr Klein in NFB cutting room during the '70s

We made films about women's history, heroes, art, and controversial issues like abortion and spirituality, and were integral to the women's movement. Our films were both inspired by and inspiring to women in Canada and elsewhere. Despite that, Studio D was marginalized and poorly supported by the Film Board. On the one hand we were producing films of relevance, films that, every time the Board was threatened, it was our films—and the support of our constituencies—that saved it. On the other hand, our films were not considered real films by the guys, or by management. Many of our films were "talking heads" of "ordinary women." We criticized the fact that the technical departments were all male, because a film about abortion or violence against women had to have a female crew. There were no women camera operators or sound recordists. All that had to change. We made waves and weren't popular. Nonetheless, *If You Love This Planet* was made by Terre Nash in Studio D, and won an Oscar. And my own film *Not a Love Story* was one of the most widely distributed films in NFB history.

I didn't know what I was getting into with *Not a Love Story*. The NFB's financial year was ending with a surplus, and money was suddenly available to make film or it would go back to the government. I had been in a cornershop with my daughter Naomi, who was about nine at the time, and seen those tits-and-ass magazines surrounding her. It set me thinking about their influence on people, and what it said about men's attitudes towards women. Why had I never thought of it before? And mostly, what might Naomi think about her own body when confronted by these images? There was a documentary there, but I really was totally ignorant of where the quest would lead. Like most women, I knew little about the sex industry. It turned out that much worse was out there than that on the covers of girlie magazines. My producer, Dorothy Hénaut, and I began our research like two Alices in Wonderland. People in New York gave us answers to our innocent questions, but in Canada nobody would talk to us, neither the pornographers, nor the feminists—it was not yet a feminist issue. *Not a Love Story* was definitely political, and reactions were polarized. In the Film Board we were told by the head of distribution that the film could not be distributed because the material was so explicit—it is extremely explicit, but not titillating. Critical and personal reactions were split along gender lines. Kathleen Shannon was absolutely clear—our films were made by women, for women, about women. If men appreciated them that was wonderful, but they were not our primary audience. Most women, myself included, had not seen real pornography, had not wanted to see it.

The format of *Not a Love Story* goes back and forth between quite explicit images; starting with advertising on billboards, progressing through violent pornography, ultimately to snuff movies with real children in third-world countries. All this is intercut with feminists, Margaret Atwood poetry, Kate Millett erotica, and all kinds of stuff which shows women grappling with the issues—it is both scary and empowering for women. But men are divided; some feel strange and guilty, some feel "we're not like that," and most feel uncomfortable. I always wondered if there was a way I could have made as strong a statement and been more inclusive of men who saw themselves as our allies— I still can't answer that question. The film started out to be about sex from a feminist point of view. But we soon realized that a film about eroticism was co-opted by the prevalence of advertising clichés and pornographic images. It was as if the language of sexuality had been kidnapped or hijacked. We discovered during the screenings that lots of women were forced to watch pornography. Some women were so shaken by our film that afterwards we found them in the washroom trying to recuperate. Even now people tell me, "That film changed my life." It was a litmus test for their relationships. The question for me, directing the film, was how much pornography to show. From our screenings I was able to strike a balance between too little for audiences who didn't know what it really was, and too much because the emotional impact was too great to handle—an interesting edit job.

I felt the need to have an articulate woman from the world of pornography as a guide, and discovered Linda Lee Tracy. She was reluctant at first, but we developed a strong relationship. She was beginning her own feminist exploration and had already met a US group called Women Against Pornography. She was also writing poetry. Linda Lee was clearly not a victim, so I would not be voyeuristic or condescending. She had a huge amount to teach me, and we became sisters—her word. I agreed from the outset that she had the right to say, and do, what

Linda Lee Tracy
*Not a Love Story*, 1981

Muriel Duckworth (left), Marion Dewar
(center), and Margaret Lawrence (right)
*Speaking Our Peace*, 1985

she did or didn't want in the film, including the edit. At first the NFB office in the States said it wasn't distributable. Then they got a theatrical distributor who pressed for it to be longer, meaning they wanted more pornography. We refused, and made the final running time an awkward 69 minutes—longer than a television-hour because I didn't trust the medium, and didn't want people to see it in isolation. A couple of years later, when the dust had settled, I agreed for it to be shown on one of the public channels followed by a panel discussion.

After *Not a Love Story* I co-directed a film with Terre Nash called *Speaking Our Peace: A Film about Women, Peace, and Power*. It was the height of the Cold War and the nuclear threat. Frankly, I was overwhelmed by the material and felt the world was about to destroy itself. We never quite figured out how to tell the story, find the metaphors, and structure it. A great subject, great women, but not a great film. Meanwhile my son Seth had been involved in anti-war work himself as part of an organization called Students Against Global Extermination (SAGE). In 1986, when he graduated high school, he and three other teenagers decided to take a year off to talk to students about peace in as many high schools as possible. I thought it was an inspiring idea, great to see youth so empowered,

and said if you can get this together, I will make a film about it. They raised the money, bought a used station-wagon, and set off across Canada. I think they spoke in 350 schools from Newfoundland to Victoria. The title, *Mile Zero*, was taken from a marker at the western end of the cross-Canada highway. At first no one in the NFB would touch the project. I began shooting on my Visa card, and then raised private money to co-produce with the NFB, who ultimately came on board. We shot it and got as far as viewing the rushes with the editor Sidonie Kerr, when I had a stroke—I was 46. It was a mild stroke, but two weeks later I had a second catastrophic one and became quadriplegic and locked in—I was hospitalized over seven months. Sidonie, who was incredibly devoted, decided to carry on. She and Irene Angelico, the co-producer, brought video copies of the cuts home, which we worked on during my weekend furloughs from the rehabilitation institute. I could hardly speak above a whisper, and couldn't even remember the end of a sentence by the time I got to it. My universe had shrunk, I'd lost my sense of self. But the passion and optimism of the teenagers on screen to save our fragile planet became a metaphor of hope for me. I found I still had the professional skills to edit the film with my colleagues' support. This work, and the film's eventual premiere, was the key to my recovery.

**Postscript**

From the earliest moment of my stroke, friends and colleagues had said: "Someday you'll make a film about this." I was angered by this seemingly voyeuristic idea. As time went on, I understood that people are more than morbidly curious about survivor stories, they are hungry for reassurance that they could in fact cope if something catastrophic happened to them (which it inevitably will, if they live long enough). I was living a fascinating experience that the documentarian in me needed to share. I found the prospect of making a film daunting with my present limitations, so I told my story and shared my new world of disability in *Bonnie and Gladys* (Gladys is my motorized scooter), a radio series for CBC. I went on to author *Slow Dance: A Story of Stroke, Love, and Disability*. The book has been described as a documentary, because it intercuts medical records, personal journals, and taped interviews with family, friends, care providers, and others with disabilities.

And 15 years post-stroke, I have not ruled out the possibility of collaborating on another documentary film…

Seth Klein
*Mile Zero: The SAGE Tour*, 1988

*Mile Zero: The SAGE Tour*, 1988

Bonnie Sherr Klein (center) during *Mile Zero: The SAGE Tour*, 1988

# Interview
# Barbara Kopple

07

### An introduction

Few documentary makers are nominated for an Oscar, fewer are awarded an Oscar, and to date only one documentary maker has two. Barbara Kopple won her first with her first film, *Harlan County, USA*, in 1977. It was 14 years later that she received a second Oscar for *American Dream*. At the 1991 Sundance Film Festival, *American Dream* won the Grand Jury Prize, the Audience Award, and the Filmmaker's Trophy. That same year *Harlan County, USA* was designated an American Film Classic by United States Congress. Kopple has also had the rare opportunity of turning the camera on the usually reclusive film director, Woody Allen, in her film *Wild Man Blues*.

# Barbara Kopple

*New York, February 4, 2003*

Everything in my parents' lives was done towards the family; they made me feel as if there was nothing I couldn't do when I was growing up, which I think gave me a sense of being able to take risks. I was born in 1946 and grew up in Scarsdale, a middle- to upper-middle class suburb of New York City. My father was in the textile business and my mother kept family and home together. My parents were democrats and we were very liberal, not religious at all; we celebrated certain holidays but we didn't discriminate between Christmas and Passover. My uncle was a playwright who wrote the play which eventually became Casablanca, based on his own experiences. I always discussed things with him so it was a proud moment for me when he came to see one of my first films and loved it.

I studied clinical psychology at North Eastern University in Boston, during which I had to do six months at Medfield Bay Hospital working with patients who'd had a lobotomy. I felt that if I wrote about it nobody would ever read it, so I made a Super8 film and thought, "This is extraordinary, it's magical." Filming it wasn't very hard because everybody was sort of media savvy and documenting things at that time. The anti-war movement was happening and there were a lot of media groups, and stuff was filmed all the time. I didn't edit the film, just showed it as it was shot, but with a commentary. I'd never venture such a thing again however.

Life is a lot about luck and timing. There was a woman in a class I took in *cinéma vérité* back in New York City, who worked for the Maysles Brothers. She told me they needed help and was I interested. I said absolutely, and they hired me and I never returned to the *vérité* class. I got the job doing everything nobody else wanted to do, which I did with great relish. At night the assistant editor left me work because I really wanted to learn the craft. I worked with the Maysles Brothers on *Gimme Shelter* in 1970, running after Albert and David with camera magazines in my arms. They treated everybody like part of the family, so I really felt able to contribute. At the time, there were only women working there. Then I got a job as an assistant editor with Larry Moyer. He really taught me

phenomenally. He would say, "I'm going out to lunch and I want this scene edited when I come back in an hour." So I started to understand how to tell a story through him.

Documentaries are not just about the raw side of life, not just the underbelly, but documenting the beauty and joy of what people are all about. I had a wonderful experience working on *Winter Soldier*, which Jane Fonda and Donald Sutherland raised the money for. It was just enough for stock or else we would beg, borrow, and steal from whoever would give it to us. Nobody on the crew got paid. We filmed Vietnam veterans giving testimony of what they did in Vietnam. I did sound and also worked on the editing. It was stupendous for me because it was a way of looking at these young, beautiful, innocent boys who had gone through so much in their lives. During the editing we all lived in a house we'd been donated and different Vietnam veterans would come and stay. Sometimes they'd wake in the morning still thinking they had their weapons. It was a real learning experience being with them, as well as having them watch the material that we were putting together. I was pretty young—I guess in my early twenties. I was highly motivated by meeting people and have them open up in such an incredible way, simply because we'd have a camera. Their stories were sometimes sad, or extraordinary. The whole essence of storytelling is what motivates me, getting deep into the soul of somebody and watching who they are and how they change over time. When a person says they'll allow me access into their lives, what I try to do as the filmmaker is to get them to forget I'm there and just allow them, in the best way I can, to go about living their lives.

One such film was *Wild Man Blues*, about Woody Allen's jazz tour. What made the difference with him was to remove him from the things that he knew—new situations tend to intimidate Woody a little. So I put a wireless microphone on him and just let him go. He'd play to the camera a little but usually we were so far away from him that he'd forget we were filming. And there was never any backtracking on his part; he couldn't wait to see the film and would keep calling to say, "So can I see something?" and I'd say, "No Woody, you know it's about four or five

*American Dream*, 1990

Barbara Kopple (second from right)
recording sound
*American Dream*, 1990

Barbara Kopple and cinematographer
Hart Perry
*Harlan County, USA*, 1976

Top: Funeral for a miner
*Harlan County, USA*, 1976

Above: A striking miner and
Barbara Kopple
*Harlan County, USA*, 1976

hours right now." Then he would call again and I'd say, "OK, it's down to three hours, come in and look at it." He and [his wife] Sunni were fascinated by what they were seeing. I think for him it was as if this relationship was happening and these two people were coming out of the screen and becoming real for him in an interesting way. He was laughing and they were holding each other and giggling. After it was over all he said was, "So how are you going to edit it down?" and I said, "Well that's my problem," and he said "Yes it is," and off they went.

Harlan County, USA was a pretty heavy film to make. It was also one that meant the most to me. I lived with coalminers, and came to understand what life and death was all about. At night we had to carry guns because gun thugs would come and start shooting up people's homes. I made some extraordinary friendships there. I'd never known people who lived and died by their guns. The first morning, there was a shoot out and one guy was put in hospital. Next day he was driving around in his car with a sign reading "38s AIN'T SHIT." Very different from Scarsdale where nobody had a gun, a totally different way of life; in Harlan County you had to show that you had your gun with you at all times. These people worked in what was one of the most dangerous industries in the country, where a man and woman die almost every other day from a rock fall or the inhalation of coal dust. These people were fighting to have the right to a union so they could work in a safe place and get a decent wage. And the coal operators were fighting with every ounce of energy to try to stop them. But the film had lots more in it; the history of miners, what black lung was about, what it was like for the widows of the Farmington mine explosion—a huge canvas. But it also told a personal story of the people from Harlan County. I definitely had a passion for these miners, although we tried to include as much as we could of the coal owners and operators. So yes,

the film totally sided with the coalminers because they were the people I'd spent time with, the people whose lives were at stake, and the people who were willing to give up anything for what they believed in.

The first showing of Harlan County, USA was at the New York Film Festival. I invited the miners and their wives to come and I was petrified because I thought maybe they'd think, "She's exploiting us." What if they hated it? Here I am in front of 1,500 people and what if they don't like it? But at the end we answered some questions and had a really good time. Hazel Dickens, a coalminer's daughter who did the music for the film, started playing music. We had passed out 1,000 song sheets and asked people to sing along—it was wonderful. Then Lois Scott, who's in the film and had just been elected treasurer of the Black Lung Association, started fundraising on stage. People were throwing up five and ten dollar bills. I was standing in the corner laughing and I guess Lois forgot she was wearing a mike, because she said, "Barbara, you stop laughing and start picking up that money and stuff it in your bra!" And this was in front of the entire Lincoln Center.

After Harlan County I made American Dream in Austin, Minnesota. It was a film concerned with the economic crisis in the Midwest. I'd been struggling to try to find some way of talking about what people were going through at that time. Ronald Reagan was in power and his economic policy was causing people to lose their jobs all over the country. I went to stay with a woman in Chicago who was in the forefront of setting up institutions for workers to learn new occupations, and to try to figure out what to do with their lives. She learnt of a plant closing in Worthington, Minnesota, and it seemed so intriguing that I went to see. But then I heard people on radio news shouting, "We're not going to take it anymore. We've had enough." They were in Austin,

and that's where I went to shoot American Dream. It took two years and was a very hard and difficult film to make. None of these films had any financing whatsoever so I'd apply to foundations for money. I was always struggling just to get a roll of film or camera people to work with. It was almost like they were doing a political favor to work with me. I'd be dropping one camera person off and picking up another, telling them what was going on. The whole fabric of the film was difficult as it involved the parent union and the local union fighting each other. On American Dream, as on many of my films, I produced, directed, and recorded sound. This really splits you in two. You have to figure out where the next bit of money is coming from, get people to work with you, make sure they have everything they need and also move the film forward. But I had so much energy; there was no way I was not going to be able to do it. I remember one particular call from our production office; I'd been on the picket line all morning and I was freezing, I mean my body was just trembling. They called and told me, "There's no money left in the bank." One of the people working with me threw in $100 to keep us going. For six months we'd been writing to Bruce Springsteen asking for his help, as he was doing a lot for workers at that time. I was pacing back and forth through the Union's hall and they were on the phone asking what I was going to do about it? I said, "I don't know, what am I going to do about it? I am thoroughly and utterly exhausted. I don't know." Then they called back later that day to say, "We just got a cheque for $25,000 from Bruce Springsteen." I just burst into tears, I was so happy.

The cinematographer on Harlan County, USA, Hart Perry, was the love of my life, and also the father of my son. It was wonderful to be able to work with somebody I cared so much about and was so in sync with. He left a teaching job to come and work with me in Eastern Kentucky and then on American Dream. It's the story and the people that charge my batteries when filming. Telling a story that nobody else cares about gives me energy, and when we get something really wonderful; a moment, a scene, watch somebody change, see them connect, or do something courageous, it gives me strength as a filmmaker, because I feel I'm doing justice to them. I think in every film I make people test me. In *Harlan County, USA* for example, we had promised that we would be on the picket line on a particular morning. To get there we had to drive down a mountainous road with no guardrails and our car went over the edge and landed in a ravine. The three of us were OK, so we pulled our gear out and walked a couple of miles to the picket line. People there realized that we cared. They saw that we were committed. I think participants want to know who they're opening up to, there has to be a trust between us.

*Fallen Champ* was my sixth film. Diane Sokolow, who worked at Columbia Tristar, suggested to them that nobody had ever really done a boxing film, suggested Mike Tyson as the subject, and recommended me as director. *Fallen Champ* was one of the first documentaries shown on NBC as a kind of "movie of the week," which I liked because

documentaries can be as entertaining and funny and carry the same narrative as any fiction film. At the beginning I didn't know anything about boxing whatsoever. Had I been a man, maybe I'd have had to prove something to those I interviewed, but as a woman I could ask whatever questions I wanted. Mike Tyson was then in jail for the rape of Desirée Washington and I got some flack from people saying, "Why do a film on Mike Tyson?" But I was fascinated to explore this guy and try to understand what happened to him. He had a tough upbringing; his stepfather beat his mother and he sort of tried to stand between them, and he got teased for his high voice by other kids. One day, somebody broke the neck of one of the pigeons he kept on his roof for pleasure. Tyson hit him, and that was when he realized he had strength. He was sent to several juvenile detention homes and at one of them he took an interest in boxing. Later, he was given a trainer called Teddy Atlas, and at a certain point Tyson tried to seduce a young relative of Teddy's. He held a gun at Tyson's head and said, "If you ever do that again I'm going to blow you away." Atlas was fired and a new trainer was put in his place, and I think from that moment Tyson understood that,

"Wow, if I'm going to be the heavyweight champ of the world that means I can do anything." And as he progressed, it meant that he could do anything; he could have girls, make lots of money, and buy expensive cars and houses. So I think when Desirée Washington said, "No," he didn't quite think that applied to him. There's a story underneath everything and we do stereotype people. If I can break through those stereotypes it makes me incredibly happy. It's very difficult as a filmmaker to be objective, but it's not difficult to be fair. People are so fascinating, and so many different elements of who they are and what they are about come out if you just allow them to feel relaxed and open. You have to look as hard and as deep as you can to be able to tell a story.

*Defending our Daughters* was for Lifetime, a television channel for women. It looked at the experiences of women who were in tough situations and were taking tremendous risks to be pro-active. We went to Sarajevo and filmed a woman in her seventies who told us how these young men had raped her. She'd known them as boys and used to give them plums as a child, and

Woody Allen and Barbara Kopple
*Wild Man Blues*, 1997

Woody Allen and his wife Sunni
*Wild Man Blues*, 1997

*Wild Man Blues*, 1997

*Wild Man Blues*, 1997

now she was blaming herself. She sort of came through her ordeal by recognizing that rape was used to humiliate the Muslim women in Sarajevo. It was an extraordinary experience for me. One of the soldiers whom we talked to said he had been told you had to rape at least one woman every single day. But it wasn't all just about rape. We filmed a different story in each country, like Pakistan and Egypt. A support group was set up for so many of these women who came together and talked about their experiences. They weren't left alone with their horror of what they'd gone through.

When I started on *Harlan County, USA* there was a place I went to in West Virginia called Cabin Creek. I decided to name my production company that because I never wanted to forget the experience of being in the coal fields and meeting those people. Just now we're developing a lot of documentaries; *Women on the Front* looks at young photographers and journalists working in places of crisis. When they go they're totally innocent, so it's about how they change and what they see. Then the veterans; what they've experienced, and their desire to return to a normal life. One photographer, a Russian in her twenties who came to the USA in 1981, went to Israel and was hired as a stringer for the Associated Press. The first day, she got shot and almost died. Now she's recovered and continues to take

photographs around the world. She wants to go back to find the Palestinian who shot her, let him know she's OK and what she's all about so that each person has their own story. We haven't raised the money yet but we've done some shoots anyway.

One of the lessons I have learnt is that if you want to do documentaries, you must not be persuaded to wait until you have the money, or be afraid to do it because you've never done it before. I think that if you care enough about the work you're doing, people will help you and will work with you and you can get it done. For me the biggest lesson is, when in doubt just to do it and not to be swayed by whatever is tradition or the so-called correct way to do things. You just have to go for it, and if you do, a whole different world and a whole different life opens for you.

*Conversations with Gregory Peck*, 2000

# Jørgen Leth

**08**

## An introduction

Poet on paper, poet on film, teacher, jazz journalist, acute observer of humankind; Leth's prolific career began with experimental documentaries in Copenhagen in the '60s. Refused a place at film school, where he now teaches, he is celebrated by his peers and revered by his students. His enthusiasms are wide and varied, from Chinese ping pong to bicycle racing, from studies of everyday human behavior to idiosyncratic studies of America and China. He is equally known in his native Denmark for his annual television commentaries of the Tour de France, as in his adopted home of Haïti for his reflections on its people, its politics, and its voodoo.

# Jørgen Leth

*Copenhagen, September 4 2002*

Mine was a modest home—my father worked for Danish railways as station master at Århus, my home town. My father was a modest, quiet man, well-informed, also quite courageous. During the [Second World War] years the railways were a sensitive place to be, and he was active in helping the resistance. Later, he took part in the anti-war movement. He was a big reader and consumed news and history. He always encouraged me to travel and appreciated my strange surreal poetry. My mother did not work. Early on I started writing for the school paper, and I wanted to travel. So while still at school, I hitchhiked to Italy, Spain, and Morocco. My father told me, "Don't forget to use your eyes, son." I made a deal with a local newspaper in Århus to write letters as I traveled, and made very good use of my father's advice. It was much later that I realized how much sense that sentence made for me. I never forgot to use my eyes. My father never traveled–it was too adventurous in the late '50s, at least for that social strata. So, in a way, I traveled for them and sent back postcards every single day.

I read comparative literature at the University of Århus, whilst living with my parents and sister. After the first year I dropped out. I had been writing about jazz for a local newspaper and I was editing a magazine when I got an offer to edit a weekly jazz page for Aktuelt, a social democratic newspaper in Copenhagen. It was 1959—I was just 22 years old. It was a great experience; I interviewed all the jazz musicians visiting Copenhagen: Miles Davis, Oscar Pettiford, Stan Getz, Charles Mingus, Eric Dolph, and Ornette Coleman—all the big names. I also began reporting on film, and I went to Rome to interview Antonioni and Monica Vitti. I met Godard, my all-time hero in filmmaking, although I never came to know him.

Although I was a close friend of Oscar Pettiford, who lived in Copenhagen, my first film in 1963 was about the greatest of all jazz pianists, Bud Powell. I had already published my first collection of poetry— poetry that is full of images and visual inspiration has always continued parallel to my filmmaking. Powell lived in Paris, and was a close associate of Charlie Parker, Dizzy Gillespie, and Max Roach. He

was a key figure and also a man with severe mental problems. A furious piano player, completely fantastic, innovative, a great virtuoso. When he came to Copenhagen I put together a film crew and a small amount of private money and made *Stop for Bud*, which in Danish means "stopping forbidden"— a play on words, but the film played with images and imagination, a quite surrealistic documentary in its storytelling. Although we couldn't afford sync-sound, we sold the rights to a jazz film distributor and it has since been distributed worldwide.

I worked with cameraman Ole John for many, many years. We wanted to reform film language right from the beginning; we wanted to do it contrary to every convention. We did not want to have sync-sound. We wanted simply to do it in another way, just for the sake of it. The next film I made was totally anarchic. It was so experimental I can't bear to see it anymore. We had no money, I was living in Spain with my first wife, and a cameraman friend came down with a 16mm Bolex camera. We wanted to put three different kinds of images and three different kinds of sounds together, but not sound from the action. It was just crazy. We filmed a scene with a Spanish barber, like Carl Dreyer's *La Passion de Jeanne d'Arc*, close-ups, macabre, and then the head of a musician playing, but never the hands, never the instrument, absolutely crazy. And the third element was a storyteller, seen but not heard. Nobody wanted to buy the film, but it was included in the Danish Film Institute's early collection because it was an example of experimental filmmaking at that time.

Then I had a big success with the first film I did professionally. *The Perfect Human* was inspired by the world of advertising. I was fascinated by the idea of isolating people in a totally empty, preferably white, room. Like a fashion photographer's limbo set. A man and a woman do simple acts of everyday life, he in a tuxedo, she in a silver-like dress and boots (it was 1967). And the voiceover says, "What is the perfect human doing?", "Who is he?", "Look at the perfect human and how he moves." The film was perceived and received as a kind of poetry, and became a big success at festivals, winning a lot of prizes. *The Perfect Human* was just 13 minutes long.

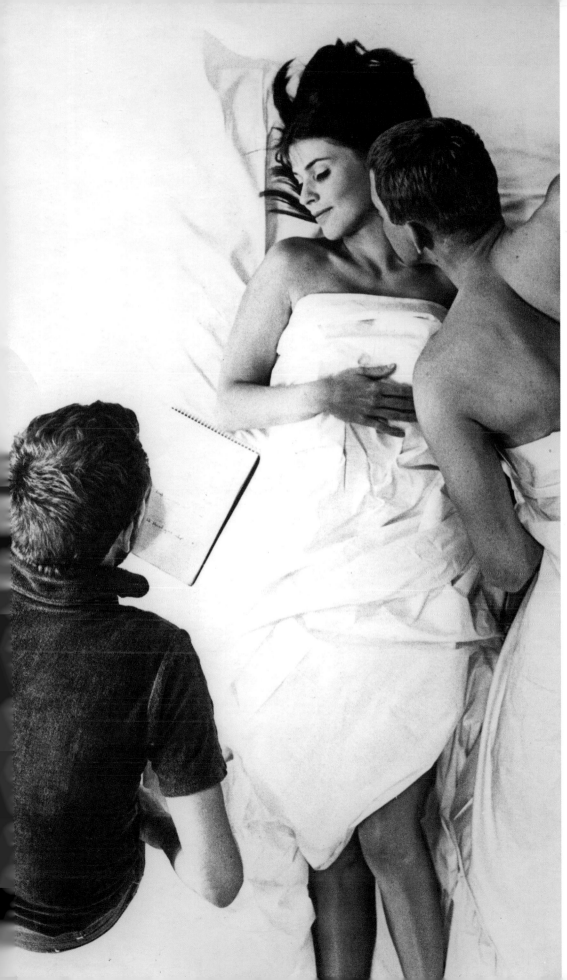

*The Perfect Human*, 1968

Andy Warhol
*66 Scenes from America*, 1982

I like going back to the concept of the empty room and did so every ten years, also with the same actors. I like to think of *The Perfect Human* as a surface which is breaking and fragmenting—I like that. I've always been fascinated to study things while they're happening, to see where they are leading. I'm totally obsessed with this whole concept of filmmaking—that you don't know the answer to your own film. That's very important. I never have the answers, I never want to give a message, I would rather keep it open, and I'd rather explore a piece of reality and see where the story leads.

From the beginning I had this controversial view of filmmaking. I was fascinated by language, and I was totally obsessed with twisting it in all ways. I had a very arrogant approach; I didn't study. My cameraman was very raw also, but he had studied, and was a photographer by profession—but me? I was a poet and just thinking film. Later, I applied to the National Film School of Denmark and I was refused. Now I have been teaching there for many years. I just learnt by doing.

I was not close to the tradition of Danish documentary, like Theodor Christensen. No, it was the opposite of what I wanted. Carl Dreyer was an idol; I still admire his work. But I was not connected with the famous Danish documentary tradition. I disliked the commentating "cut," I disliked the all-knowing editor. I was more inspired by chance, by the painter/filmmaker Andy Warhol, and the American composer John Cage. Danish documentary tradition was very old-fashioned. I disliked the whole attitude of educating people, being superior, telling people what to think. I much preferred Godard to Truffaut, for instance; Truffaut was prose, Godard was poetry.

In Copenhagen I found people who liked to experiment, and by the end of the '60s we formed a group of writers, painters, sculptors, and filmmakers called AB Cinema. At the same time others started a literary magazine. We all started to cross the borders between the arts—painters were making films, film-makers were painting, writers were participating in all kinds of things, we were in the "happening" era—very foreign to the Danish film environment. We were the avant-garde. We made collective films during the '70s; 30 to 40 people with Super8 cameras. We did some interesting experiments, I think—in the forests, a supermarket, and a portrait of the Danish Prime Minister, Jens Otto Krag, who had agreed to be a model for this kind of collective filmmaking. I think we really wanted to demonstrate that filmmaking was just a paper tiger, and anybody can do it. It takes ideas and thought, but not technical skills, definitely, and I liked that.

A common aim of my filmmaking has been to simplify and to believe in simple ways to tell stories, simple techniques but use them straight, use them clean, and with a sense of aesthetics. I invite chance into the shooting process and sometimes in the editing also. I went to China without having done any research, just with my own sensibility and my wonderful cameraman and sound man with their sensibilities. I went without preconceptions about how China was supposed to be, and shot film to observe moments. This was a pure documentary, not stylized, not stiff, just sensitive documentary filmmaking. *Notebook from China* is a collection of notes according to the itinerary. A one-hour documentary, very successful at festivals and very beautiful, I think. A relaxed piece, not the kind the BBC would make. I just felt I wanted to see China as a subjective observer. I want to follow my instincts, my curiosity, my subjective view of situations, and see what happens—thanks to considerable financial support from the Danish Film Institute.

*66 Scenes from America*, 1982

I prefer to shoot film, and I have up till now, mostly with the same cameraman Dan Holmberg, who I've worked with since 1973. He would never shoot video because of the quality. I also don't want to over-shoot, because it's important to be selective. And I like the idea of film passing through the camera, and that it costs money. I like the obligation in that idea; I'm fascinated by the magic of film, which requires to be exposed so as to be seen. But I'm aware of video and its sensibility, and in *Haïti.Untitled,* which I finished in 1995, I mixed film and DV.

I live in Haïti and shoot a lot of Hi8 myself. I closely followed events during the political crisis of the early '90s. I shot everything; the most dramatic, horrible things with my video camera—bloody bodies in the streets, voodoo ceremonies—plus a lot of private erotic material. My aim was to do a documentary on different aspects of Haïti; the politics, voodoo, sensualism, daily life, a subjective but total view. I wanted to shoot film but I did a lot on video as well, which we then edited together. I had a very good editor who liked the idea of video, and he told me to

shoot more on it. I was amazed, but there was a textural difference. After that, I have used both.

*Haïti.Untitled* was very complicated in its editing and very different from my other films. Now I want to be straightforward and use long takes and so on. Dan Holmberg has a marvelous ability to fade-out in camera by reducing the aperture. He edits in camera, determining in a way the timing of the shot. My editor respects his choices. An element of chance again, in the shooting and even the editing.

I want to make films which look good, but I don't think of the audience—well, not consciously. Sometimes I choose crazy subjects, like in *Pelota*, about a ball-game in the Basque country—I made a 47-minute film about that. So I don't think of what could be popular. When I have, I've been mistaken, like with *Michael Laudrup: A Football Player*. Sure to succeed! Big budget! Big public interest! It was too easy, and confirmed that I'm right to select challenges and make them more difficult each time. I'm intrigued by the way words connected to images can change the content and the reading of the

image. That's probably my poet background. I work with text, which is sometimes minimalistic, sometimes contradictory to the image, and sometimes questions what you see. I like that.

I don't hold principled opinions. I rely on sensibility. Lars von Trier confronted me about this on a film we're doing together called *The Five Obstructions*. He makes unpredictable moves (obstructions) on my filmmaking, which can be technical, as in the first segment, or an ethical test in the second segment. But von Trier also wanted to know what I could not, or would not, film. My list included a dying child and a murder committed on camera. I am confronting these issues in another project, *The Erotic Human*. I don't want to make pornography but I want to create very sensual scenes, so it's a question of aesthetic approach, of finding an appropriate way to tell the story. I will film even obscene parts of a voodoo ceremony, but it's a question of aesthetic strategy. I filmed a number of bodies of people murdered during the night in *Haïti.Untitled*. I found the key to filming these scenes—Chantel Regnault, a French photographer

*Haïti. Untitled,* 1996

*Haïti. Untitled*, 1996

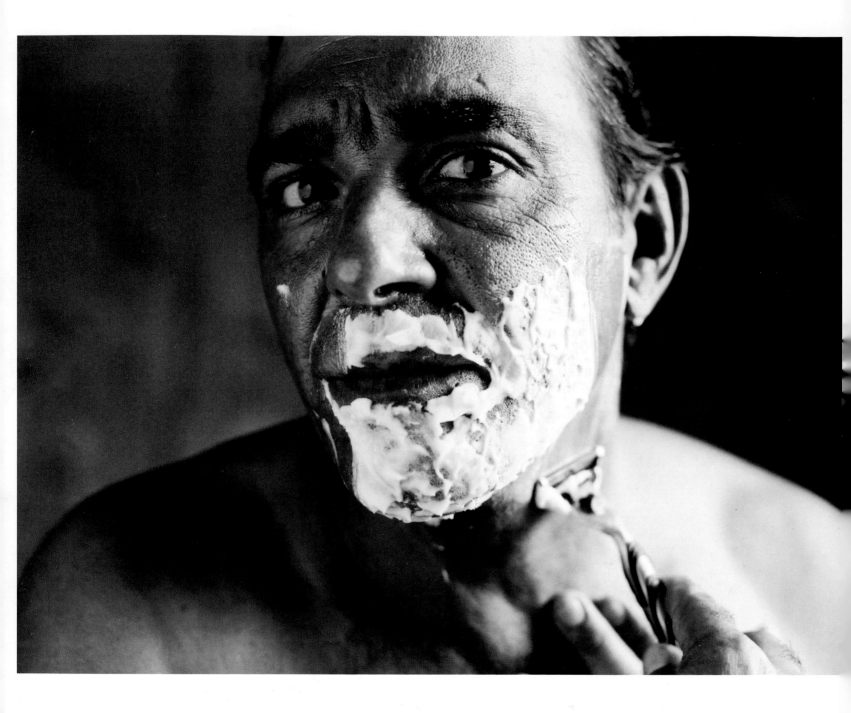

*The Five Obstructions*, currently in
production

I knew who worked in a respectful way, provided me with the vehicle—by filming Chantel photographing the corpses, I resolved my problem.

I have to feel intrigued or attracted to the subject to be interested. I'm simply following my interest in a certain phenomenon. My theory is that wherever you cut into reality or life you find the strange and the bizarre. My experience is that when I delve into a subject I find something more, something deeper, about life itself. Objectivity is an illusion. I go after what I'm attracted to and try to tell it as precisely as I can, with personal engagement. That's my aim, always. I believe that if you observe intensely, enough things reveal themselves out of nearly nothing.

I have not experienced direct censorship, only in an unspoken form. *Notebook from China* is a poetic, impressionistic film with absolutely no political substance or opinion, just the beauty of the landscapes and people. We were lucky enough to have a guide from the Chinese Ministry who saw things from our point of view. But the Ministry didn't like the finished film, nor did the Chinese Embassy, when it was shown here. Why hadn't I filmed some factories, some modern stuff instead of all that old-fashioned and poor stuff? On *Haïti.Untitled* I had problems of a different kind. The elite Haïtians don't want to see their villains, or the misery, or to be confronted with the voodoo. There's a lot of hypocrisy in Haïti. So I don't show the film there anymore.

The relationship between Dan Holmberg and me is based on confidence, total confidence. He knows what I like. We agree on aesthetics. Given the many years we've worked together, there have been very few moments of crisis. He prefers not to be disturbed by me telling him something during a shot; that would disturb the participants anyway. He always has his left eye open and knows how to frame a shot. I trust him completely. I have the same level of confidence with my editor, Camilla Skousen. The degree of trust with Camilla has got to the point where I am rarely in the editing suite. I see all the rushes, make a note of things I like, and with a list of the scenes we compare our lists. Mostly we agree on what must be in the film. We never kill the "darlings"; we always keep the "darlings." Camilla works in Denmark while I am away in Haïti. Last winter she edited *New Scenes from America*. My producer Marianne Christensen and Camilla came to Haïti with the first cut. I don't give Camilla a cutting order, not even the first or last scenes. So I'm always excited about what she's going to show me. I trust her sense of telling. On the first showing I had tears in my eyes. After she left, I had second thoughts. September 11 happened while we were shooting in the States, but the film had no reference to New York's post-9/11 skyline—a delicate problem. Where to place it? How to show it? At the end? I just wanted to hint subtly at what had happened. I told Camilla this and she sent me three or four different cuts and then it was there. Some of my colleagues are shocked by this kind of long-distance editing.

A lesson I've learnt is that I should not relax by making films that are too easy. I should always take on either an extremely difficult subject like *The Erotic Human* or a way of telling a story that poses real challenges, as with *The Five Obstructions*. That's a lesson, that's an eternal lesson for me. Maybe I have inspired people to see something in unknown territories, to use their imagination, even to interpret phenomena that they encounter in their daily lives; different, strange realities. I am a stubborn person and believe very much in what I'm doing, never in doubt. And I believe in my right to do the most strange and bizarre films with no appeal to a wider audience. I am grateful to the cultural context here in Denmark, especially to the Film Institute for their understanding.

Left: *The Five Obstructions*,
currently in production

Above: Jørgen Leth
*The Five Obstructions*,
currently in production

# Errol
# Morris

**09**

### An introduction

Self-proclaimed "contrarian," 40 years a cellist, 30 years a filmmaker and one-time private detective, Morris has crossed the great divide between documentary essayist and commercials director. As a documentary maker all his works have been screened in cinemas across the USA, and on television in many countries around the world.

As a highly successful director of commercials he produces for America's leading brand names Morris is the epitome of the anti-*vérité* school, taking his unique style of documentary to extraordinary lengths, such as the invention of his awesome-sounding Interratron machine.

# Errol Morris

*Paris, January 9 and 16 2003*

I went from seeing hardly any movies to compulsively seeing many, many, many movies, one movie after another after another. I decided I wanted to make my own. I had worked on one as an assistant to Werner Herzog, a movie that he shot partly in the United States. Not so long after that, I decided to make my own movie, *Gates of Heaven*, which was finished in 1978—it's my first film. And it is a very strange film, I am very proud of it. I still like it after all these years.  This is the story of two pet cemeteries, a successful pet cemetery and an unsuccessful pet cemetery. And it's a story that goes well beyond where the story is set—it becomes a kind of phantasmagoria about America.

On the one hand I would call it a documentary film, on the other hand I would call it a reaction to prevailing ideas about how documentary should be made, what documentary should look like. I'm a kind of contrarian, and there was something very contrary about the idea of *Gates of Heaven*. There is a tendency to think of documentary or non-fiction as being "one thing," and in fact it's not that at all. It's quite heterogeneous, it's quite diverse, and it is on some level experimental filmmaking. And hence often the rules are made up as you go along, and there are many, many different kinds of rules. When I started making *Gates of Heaven*, I had seen a lot of *cinéma vérité*, principally films by Fred Wiseman. But the *vérité* style, as I imagine it, is the idea that the camera is not interacting with the world, it's merely observing—the so-called fly on the wall; available light, hand-held camera, the camera crew should be as unobtrusive as possible, so on and so forth. And *Gates of Heaven* came out of a desire to do almost the exact opposite; instead of being as unobtrusive as possible, being as obtrusive as possible. In fact, you know a good part of the film is people addressing the camera. You could even say in some real sense they're performing for camera,

they are real people but they are delivering a performance. Instead of hand-held camera and available light, I lit everything, and the camera was on a tripod.

There are all kinds of conventions that we take for granted—that this is the way we're supposed to do things. And what happens if you just look at those conventions and reject them and try something quite different? What if you simply eschew the idea of interviewing people? What happens?

One of the contrarian elements of *Gates of Heaven* was that everyone was looking into the camera, and the interview situation is supposed to be one of those examples where perhaps you want to break that rule. Most interviews—when you start to think about how an interview is done and recorded on film—are done *vérité* style. Let me explain. If the *vérité* idea is the fly-on-the-wall idea, where you're observing something but not interacting with it per se, you film an interview by showing two people talking to each other; they're looking at each other, but they're not looking at you or at your camera. Well, imagine a completely different idea of putting an interview together, an idea where the person is looking directly at the interviewer and directly into the lens of the camera at the same time. Why? Why bother? Well, for several reasons. One of the central features of how we communicate with each other is eye contact. And we all know it's part of the wiring of our brains that eye contact is extremely important—how we look at each other; how we make eye contact; break eye contact; look at each other; look away from each other; it's something endowed with enormous content. But that's lost in the *vérité* style recording of an interview. I mean, yes, you're aware of one person looking at another person, but that moment of connection and disconnection, as we would experience it in a conversation with another person, is lost.

*Gates of Heaven*, 1977

Dramatized reconstructions
*The Thin Blue Line*, 1988

*Gates of Heaven*, 1977

This idea of style versus the underlying content of a film. The one point that I was clear about, even during the making of *Gates of Heaven*, is that there was a metaphysical claim in *cinéma vérité*—the claim that this was, just as the name implies, truth cinema. That by virtue of shooting things in a certain way, we were doing something that was more truthful than doing it in some other way—pick this style and ye shall know the truth. And there was something that I felt then, and still feel now, that was deeply confused at best and simply wrong about that belief—that truth is not guaranteed by style. It's not by virtue of doing something in a certain way that truth emerges. Any kind of style doesn't guarantee the truth. This is even aside from issues about the truth of images as opposed to truth as I understand it, which is something intimately connected with the use of language, and not necessarily the use of pictures.

I have, what I would call, an "obsessive concern"— it's something that runs through every film that I've made—this obsessive concern with language. I had started interviewing people, really before I became a filmmaker. Everywhere I went I took my tape recorder and I developed a style, a very definite style of interviewing. I became involved in

doing something very, very different. I became interested in getting people to talk, getting people to create if not a complete monologue, something leaning away from dialogue to monologue, the extended soliloquy.

I developed this two-minute rule during the making of *Gates of Heaven*; that if you leave people alone and let them talk without interrupting them, in two minutes they will show you how crazy they really are. That proved to be the case again and again and again and again and again during the making of that film.

There's an interview in *The Thin Blue Line* that I'm very, very proud of. I'm proud of a whole number of the interviews, but I'm proud of this interview in particular. One of the eyewitnesses on the roadway was a woman named Emily Miller, and Emily Miller was the platinum blonde eyewitness who was passing by—was seated in the passenger seat of a car (her husband was driving)—and claimed to have seen everything. I would say that it's an example of the power of this kind of thing that I do, the power of this very simple kind of method. She started talking— there are lines in my films that I think are just so crazy, it justifies to me what I'm doing, it

makes sense to me as an explanation of why I continue on with this. Emily Miller said to me, "Everywhere I go, you know, everywhere I go there's murders, even round my house." She said that she had watched a lot of detective shows on television. She loved, in particular, these shows about *Boston Blackie*, and her dream when she was a little girl was being a detective or the wife of a detective, as she puts it. She also told me out of nowhere—this is not in response to some adversarial question, nor my attempt to trick her or to show her up as a liar, or to prove that she committed perjury during trial because I was simply letting her talk—she starts talking about the police line-up where she supposedly identified the guy who was convicted, if you like, "the fall guy," Randall Adams. And she says, "You know, I picked out the wrong guy, because he had changed his physical appearance. He was looking at me funny, I didn't like the way he was looking at me, the way he was looking at me scared me, it was making me nervous." I said nothing, but she went on at enormous length trying to justify why she had failed to pick him out in this police line-up, forgetting all the while that she had testified to the exact opposite at the murder trial. At some point I asked her, "You picked out the wrong man? How did you know you picked out the wrong man?"

*Fast, Cheap, and Out of Control*, 1996

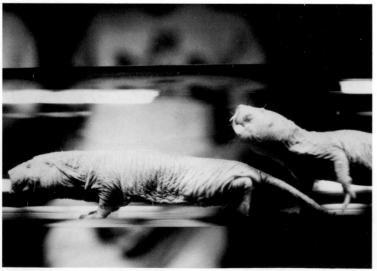

*Stairway to Heaven*, 1998

And she said, "I know." And I said, "Well, how did you know?" She said, "I know because the policeman sitting next to me told me I had picked out the wrong man and then pointed out the right man so I would not make that mistake again."

The unscripted things people say on camera then become the script for what I later film. The filming, if you like, has two parts to it; creating the interviews, thinking about the interviews and then figuring out how to create a visual element around them.

The visual element to the movie can be quite independent of the interview material, and that is shot in a way that employs elements of *vérité*. Certainly, when you see the gardener (from *Fast, Cheap, and Out of Control*) trimming his topiary garden, some of that is what I would call "traditional *vérité*" footage. There is material, for example, where you see him catch a fly with one hand while he's busy with his hand shears, and that's *vérité* in the classic sense—it's a camera that is observing and recording spontaneously unscripted things. But there are other elements (in *Fast, Cheap, and Out of Control*) which are quite the opposite. The final scenes in the movie show the gardener walking through the garden in the rain and there's mist. But these last scenes are shot at 150 frames per second—it's severely over-cranked—there are three rain towers, fog machines, huge lights on condors. This was shot near midnight in the garden where it was necessary not only to light the garden, but to light it for slow-motion photography, which means that it was lit many, many times brighter than it

would just be for normal photography. A friend of mine that was looking at this spectacle—there's 50 people on the crew creating this—said, "This may be the fly on the wall, but it's a 500-pound fly on the wall." And it's playing with these kinds of ideas, which I think is an essential part of what I do.

I've been told that I am the progenitor of a host of reality-based shows with re-enactments because of the re-enactments of the crime which appeared in *The Thin Blue Line*. They have been endlessly imitated in I don't know how many, many, many movies, in both dramatic films, documentary films, television shows, and so on and so forth. But it's interesting to me that the re-enactments in *The Thin Blue Line* were intended to be ironic in this sense; that they were illustrations of untruth, of confusions, deceptions, error. They were part of an extended essay on the theme of how believing often can be seeing and not the other way round—illustrations, not of reality, but of phantasmagoria. And I like to think that every one of my films is an exploration of that. You could think of film in general, and you can certainly think of documentary film as being an attempt to deal with that issue of what's out there, what is real and what is imagined, a Cartesian essay if you like.

To me, people can become involved in endless debates about what the difference is between fact-based filmmaking—so-called documentary—and fiction filmmaking. To me, it's not so much about documentary versus drama, because there is no clear line between the two, it is between the

controlled and uncontrolled. It amuses me that people have said about *The Thin Blue Line*, "Well, this is not a documentary because Errol Morris has staged all of these scenes, there are all of these re-enactments, there are all of these elements of drama in the middle of this documentary film, and it's not a documentary as a result." And I guess the further point is that somehow what the movie is saying is suspect as a result, but there is no kind of filmmaking that gives you truth on a platter. It's an attempt to provide an investigation of what's out there and the results of pieces and parts of that investigation have been put together, along with an essay about the nature of evidence. I like to think that every film I've made makes us fall back and ask ourselves questions about the nature of what we know about the world and how we know it.

So re-enactments or no re-enactments, when someone sits down in front of my camera, Emily Miller for example, or eventually the kid who I believe was the real killer, the words that they're saying are not words that I have scripted, they're extemporaneous. They may be performing for the camera. In fact, of course they're performing for the camera. They're aware that I'm there—they're talking to me, they're performing for me in the same sense that an actor in a drama performs for the director and for that imagined audience that eventually is going to be watching the film. There is an element of performance, but there is also an element of reality.

*Mr Death: The Rise and Fall of Fred A Leuchter Jnr*, 1999

# Anand Patwardhan

10

### An introduction

Racial, religious, and extreme political intolerance are Anand Patwardhan's preoccupations. Although not intended as a history of modern India, his films are a chronicle of India since independence, a society dominated by the bigotry of both Hindus and Muslims. Patwardhan has struggled through his documentaries to alert the world to the dangers of a growing polarization in his country. Over the past 20 years Patwardhan has produced documentaries that examine in minute detail the clash between classes, genders, faiths, and India's political parties. Equipped with the means to fight an atomic war, her explosive condition is cause for serious concern, which Patwardhan makes the subject of his latest work, *War and Peace*. As his own producer, cameraman, interviewer, and editor, all self-taught, Patwardhan's strength derives from his perseverance, compassion, and extraordinary insight into the human condition.

# Anand Patwardhan

*Paris, January 9 and 16, 2003*

My family was active in the non-violent freedom movement led by Mahatma Gandhi, especially two of my uncles, who spent years in jail under British rule. But my own politicization really began only when I went on scholarship to Brandeis University in the USA in 1970, and got involved in the anti-Vietnam War movement. I was arrested a couple of times and after graduation, worked as a volunteer with Cesar Chavez's United Farm Workers' Union in California.

I fell into filmmaking by accident. At Brandeis I studied sociology and had no formal film training, but was able to borrow film equipment and learn by trial and error—more error than trial at first—in order to shoot footage of anti-Vietnam War protests. My first completed short film was made to raise money for refugees who were crossing into India from East Pakistan (later to become Bangladesh). We asked everyone in the university to fast for a day and donate the money for the refugees. The excuses people made that day for not fasting were intercut with photographs of extreme hunger to make a fundraiser called *Business as Usual.*

In 1972 I returned to India and did voluntary work in a village, farming, teaching science and Hindi, and film was far from my mind. Once, because a neighboring center had a tuberculosis clinic in which patients needed to understand that TB requires long-term aftercare, I took up a still camera and cassette recorder to make a filmstrip for out-patients. In 1974–75 I joined a non-violent, anti-corruption movement in Bihar. One of my tasks was to take photographs of police repression, but I recruited a friend with a Super8 camera to film a demonstration that faced violent attacks from the police. Another friend later shot footage with an old hand-cranked Bell & Howell 16mm camera, but we had no synchronous sound. We projected the Super8 onto a screen and filmed that with a 16mm camera to achieve a "blow up." From all this material I managed to make a half-hour film called *Waves of Revolution*. As the film neared completion, an "Emergency" was declared in India and people we had filmed were arrested. The state crushed the movement—there was martial law, no freedom of speech, people were jailed for just talking on a train. The film went underground. I cut it in pieces and

smuggled it abroad. A few months later I took up an old offer to do a Masters degree in Canada, pieced *Waves of Revolution* back together, and screened it outside India in protest against the Emergency.

Fortunately the Emergency ended in 1977 and I returned to India. My next film, *Prisoners of Conscience*, was about political prisoners. A new government had come to power, promising to restore civil liberties, but many accused of being Communists remained locked up. I had interviewed people released from prison, but the film now became concerned with political prisoners still in jail after the Emergency.

In the early 1970s I was influenced by Latin American filmmakers fighting neo-colonialism and their ideas about "imperfect cinema"—a cinema that proudly bore the marks of the struggles they depicted. If the raw stock was outdated and grainy, the film scratched, or some shots out of focus and hurried, it did not lessen the impact of what was being said. My own zero-budget work lived up to these "low" aesthetic standards, and I was happy to make a virtue of necessity.

Legibility has always been more important to me than the "look" of things. Being self-taught, it took time for my camerawork to improve. Over the years I became better, but I still never cut in shots just because they look good, unless they help with clarity in some way. This is not to say that every shot must have an immediately recognizable function, but I'm suspicious about art for art's sake and impatient with self-conscious "art." To me the best art occurs without one's knowledge, as a by-product of one's work, from the integrity of what's on screen.

Initially mostly others did camera for me, like Pradeep Krishen in *Waves of Revolution* and Martin Duckworth in *A Time to Rise. Bombay Our City* was the turning point. I had just bought a secondhand 16mm camera, but was not yet confident. Meanwhile the homes of the urban poor of Bombay were being bulldozed in an attempt to "beautify" the city. Ranjan Palit, a young graduate from the Film Institute in Pune, not only volunteered to shoot more than a third of *Bombay Our City* without salary;

Street dwellers
*Bombay Our City*, 1985

*Bombay Our City*, 1985

he also helped me to overcome my own shyness about shooting. Ranjan's work in the film is outstanding, and he went on to become one of India's most sensitive and intuitive documentary camerapersons. Later, partly for reasons of economy, I began to shoot more myself. My films were unplanned and shot over a very long time, making it expensive (by now I had started paying salaries!) and difficult to tie down a cameraperson. Shooting myself also helped economize with raw stock. On long interviews, for instance, I knew when to turn the camera off and then on again. What started out of necessity soon became enjoyable. I've grown to like the direct eye contact that is achieved when one shoots and interviews at the same time. There are advantages and disadvantages of being both cameraperson and editor. By narrowing down the point of view one can get more focused, but one can lose out on crucially tangential moments. Sometimes I miss the joy of discovering a new viewpoint; at other times I'm thankful that the shot I really wanted is there without the filter of someone else's eye.

I mostly work with a tiny crew of people who have worked with me for many years—usually close friends. Payment comes in at some point, but the film comes first, and has to be made with whatever is in the bank. When the film recovers its costs, further money is recycled into the next film. I don't look for funding and I don't write proposals, and don't know even after filming starts where it's going to take me. I don't have a high motivation to continue making films for the hell of it, and so new projects begin only when events and ideas begin to oppress me too much. Another reason I'm reluctant to seek grant money is that my films are often critical of the state, and I don't want to be accused later of being funded from the "outside." We record things of interest until it becomes a critical mass and begins to look like it could become a film. *War and Peace*, my most recent film, took 3 1/2 years to make. At the time there were other events we were also filming, but India's nuclear tests and their aftermath became more immediate and everything else got left on the back burner. Very occasionally more than one film gets made concurrently. This

happened with *Father, Son and Holy War* (made between 1986 and 1995) and *A Narmada Diary* (1990–95) and was possible because a colleague, Simantini Dhuru, did the major camerawork on the latter film. In the Narmada valley, indigenous and other affected people are heroically resisting the construction of a gigantic dam that will drown their fertile fields and homes. Our film, shot in Hi-8, is a video diary of five years of this ongoing struggle.

Making a film is only half the battle. Showing these films is the real thing. Otherwise, what's the use of spending all this time and energy? If I didn't personally screen my films and talk to audiences I think I'd lose my motivation for making them. But I believe films can have a real political impact only if they reach mass audiences; in other words, through television. Even if I were to screen a film every day of my life with my own traveling projector, it would still be seen by less than 1 percent of India's population. The Indian state doesn't easily tolerate criticism, so I'm constantly fighting court battles to force the national television network to show my

Street dwellers
*Bombay Our City*, 1985

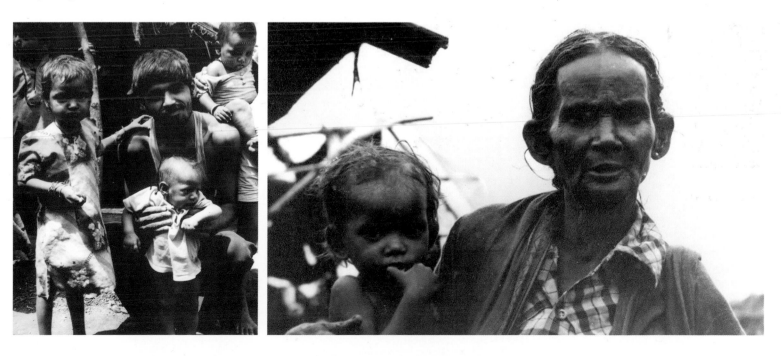

work. We succeeded on three occasions. *Bombay Our City* was the first case. Although it won a National Award for Best Documentary in 1985, the government television channel, Doordarshan, rejected it. I went to Bombay's High Court to argue for my right to freedom of speech and the public's right to information. Doordarshan's mandate is to show the best documentaries, so it was caught out and we won. On the same grounds we also won with *In Memory of Friends*, a film on communal strife in Punjab, and again with *In the Name of God*, on the rise of Hindu fundamentalism. Recently with *Father, Son and Holy War*, we won in the Bombay High Court again but suffered a setback in the Supreme Court. Today the right-wing Hindu fundamentalist ideology is slowly but surely undermining the checks and balances of our democratic system, but the case isn't completely lost. It probably means many more years will pass before this film gets to the public at large.

While politics is responsible for my films being unwelcome on television stations at home, abroad it is the dumbing down of television in general that has achieved the same result. Thought isn't on the agenda now and my films require some thought, not a lot, but at least an interest in things happening outside the immediate vicinity. In America, for instance, they're hardly interested in anything that's happening to people elsewhere in the world unless they happen to bomb them or be bombed by them. British television was briefly better, when people like Alan Fountain encouraged the idea that the "South" (those from the developing world) could make films about their own countries, rather than people from the "North" (the well-off countries) parachuting in for five days and flying home with their story.

I'm not much into cinema "theory." I find it self-congratulatory and limiting and subject to the vagaries of fashion. Take the notion of "self-reflexivity" or "democracy of form." There is no getting away from the fact that filmmaking is manipulative and the filmmaker retains control in over a hundred different ways. Even the famous "jump-cut" is merely a statement. It's the director's way of saying: "I'm not trying to manipulate you." But manipulation does not begin and end with the seamless cut. One is always choosing to use one camera angle over another, and deciding from amongst so many variables. The ultimate truth of a film does not depend on formalistic gestures, but lies in a realm between the filmmaker and his conscience.

When I started in the early '70s, there was no video. Video freed me to shoot a lot more than I would on film, because film is so expensive and I've had many horror stories with it. Video is more foolproof. I do have a tendency to overshoot on video and then have the nightmare of editing vast amounts of material that is all over the place, but this also makes the films more multi-dimensional than before. Films like *In the Name of God* and *Father, Son and Holy War* were on celluloid and had shooting ratios of 8:1 at the most. *War and Peace* was made on DV with a ratio of over 100:1. Video also automatically provides you with synchronous sound, which is more amenable to what, at times, is a single-person shooting unit. There are people who still swear by celluloid but, frankly, I feel it's old hat to worry about film or video because the quality of video has improved to such an extent that in cinemas equipped with a good video projector, you can hardly tell them apart. My projected DV footage of today looks a lot better than the best 16mm projections ever did. As for the new technical advances, although I use non-linear editing, my habits were formed in film, so I'm a bit of a purist. I almost never use dissolves, preferring straight cuts, not much layering, no background music, few audio tracks, and very little color correction.

Poster glorifying Sati (left) and
the film's poster (right)
*Father, Son and Holy War*, 1995

Freedom fighter Bhagat Singh, hung
at the age of 23 by the British
*In Memory of Friends*, 1990

These films are made over long periods of time and until I really have a crucial aspect of the story, I don't end it. That's the advantage of not being commissioned, not having a deadline. Shooting and editing are often simultaneous—it's an ongoing process. And when the structure is almost in place the narration begins to shape itself. I prefer not to use narration, but this has been achieved only rarely. *Bombay Our City* (82 minutes) dealt with Bombay's street dwellers and the city's elite that live in apartments. In a sense it was a dialogue on film between inhabitants of a city who in reality don't actually talk or listen to each other. Narration wasn't necessary as the contrasts were so stark, and everything became clear by just seeing and hearing the participants. In other films the issues are more complex and the story won't tell itself, so I fill in the links. Narration provides a framework to understand the unfolding story, but even in *War and Peace* intervention is limited. This was the first time I used a first-person narrative. I felt the need to start with my family background—something I wouldn't normally volunteer, because I knew that a film that critiques jingoism and the flag would inevitably be accused of being unpatriotic. So I established my

"national" credentials crudely by stating that my family fought for independence. What remains an irony is that the Hindu fundamentalists in power today who accuse me of being a traitor, belong to the ideology that killed Gandhi. Not only that, but instead of fighting for independence, they supported the British, as did Muslim fundamentalists. Those who fought for our independence wanted a secular, democratic society, and that's what the film is about—nostalgia for the ideals of independence and grief for what has happened to them today.

The risks I face as a filmmaker are minimal compared to the fact that there have been times when people with strong convictions who spoke out on camera paid for this with their lives. The Hindu priest who spoke out against Hindu fundamentalism in *In the Name of God*, was the priest of the temple later demolished by Hindu mobs. He had, of course, spoken out many times in the press before I filmed him—he was a very brave man. After the film was completed I showed it to him and asked if now that he was on film, things could become more dangerous for him. He laughed

and said, "You're doing my work for me." He thanked me and took tapes to screen in his temple town of Ayodhya. A year later he was killed. I felt terrible. I felt a sense of failure and shame on the part of all the secular forces in our country that we couldn't protect him. The failure was not that he was on film, but that he wasn't enough on film and in the mainstream media. He was one of the heroes of secular India, but even after he was murdered news of his death appeared only in a small column on the inside pages of a few newspapers. Had he been famous, it would have been much more risky for anybody to kill him.

Although I am outspoken, the risks I take are far smaller than those taken by some of the people I have filmed. I'm protected by my class and caste, by the fact that people know and support me. So I have a responsibility to use my privileged position to speak out against fundamentalism. If a Muslim did this, he'd be finished. Nor can a working-class person do as I can. In my last few films I lay stress on the rise of Hindu fundamentalism because I see it as a growing danger in India. More than 80 percent of Indians are Hindu, and when a majority

*In the Name of God*, 1992

becomes fundamentalist, genocide can happen. Whereas Muslim fundamentalism and militancy in India is a form of suicide—when Muslims commit some crazy act against Hindus, ten Muslim lives are taken for every Hindu death. I'm obviously opposed to all fundamentalism, but in my part of the world, and probably elsewhere, religious fundamentalism is more "politics" than "religion." I have no quarrel with Hindus, Muslims, or any groups that are genuinely religious. Violence begins when religion is used for political power. I'm not personally religious but can see the good in many religions, including my own. But I also see religion as an instrument of power in the hands of an elite that guards its privilege while others toil in illusion.

Occasionally I'm tempted by the idea of doing fiction to tell the story of people no longer alive or of times gone by. But the greatest temptation of fiction is, of course, the undeniable fact that fiction has the chance of theater release and of being seen by millions, while documentary tragically remains a marginal input in the psyche of the world. Possibly it's a failure of nerve, perhaps I don't have the skills

to do fiction—I definitely don't have the managerial skills to run a large production. I also find it hard to delegate—that's why I end up doing so many things myself. But there are also many positive reasons for sticking to documentaries. They empower the real people they are about. They have value as historical evidence and record. Who would believe that Hitler's death camps existed if we did not have the actual footage? Who would believe that Hindu mobs poured petrol on small children in Gujarat and set them alight? Who would believe that in the '70s Ronald Reagan's advisor Brezhinsky, addressing Muslim children in Pakistan, preached the gospel of "Jehad" (Islamic Holy War)? And if not for the documentary, instead of images of Gandhi, would we not have to suffice with those of Ben Kingsley?

Anand Patwardhan (right) presenting
one of his documentaries

Left: *A Time to Rise*, 1981
Right: Film poster
*In the Name of God*, 1992

# Jean-Marie Teno

11

### An introduction

Although now living in France, Jean-Marie Teno's documentaries take as their substance Cameroon's rite of passage from an agrarian to a semi-industrial nation. He sees the scars of colonization first by Germany, then Britain, and, before independence in 1960, by France. Teno belongs to a generation of African filmmakers committed to awakening audiences to colonialism, neo-colonialism, migration, dictatorship, and the abuse of power. In his view, "colonization, civilization, independence, then humanitarian talk are merely excuses and theatrical gestures to ensure that Africa remains the place which foreign powers can exploit with a good conscience." In *Africa, I Will Fleece You* Teno's off-screen voice explains, "I sought the relationship of cause and effect between the unbearable past, with its colonial violence, and the present. I sought the reason why a land with well-structured traditional societies changed into an incompetent state."

# Jean-Marie Teno

*Meze, October 21 2002*

My family background is humble. I was born in 1954 and raised in the Cameroon until I was 21. In 1975, I spent a year in England at Portsmouth Polytechnic before coming here to France—a year studying electronics on a scholarship from the British Council. I met so many young political activists in international socialist groups, and was far more fascinated by their discussions than in electronics. I spent the year learning English, talking a lot, participating in debates and reading the Socialist Worker newspaper. Then I moved to France and took a Masters in communication at the University of Valenciennes. After graduating I started in television, and for almost 15 years worked as an editor. During my annual vacations I went back to the Cameroon to make short films, as I really wanted to say things about where I came from, about my country. Eventually the films were so demanding that I had to take first three, then six months off. In the end, I quit to produce and direct full-time.

The television job was just a means of earning a living. With the first payment of my salary I bought a 16mm camera. All I really wanted to do was to make films, and because I didn't go to film school I learnt by practicing and reading, and trying to understand how they are made. I was a one-man crew. I had been a good student, and my family hoped I'd become a doctor or an engineer and be able to support them. So when I turned out to be a filmmaker, spending all my money, not earning much of it, it was something of a disappointment for them. I'm the oldest of seven—five sisters and a brother. None of my family made films; none was in the arts.

Ken Loach inspired me. The way he made his films was so realistic to me. I just had the feeling of really living with these people. At the time I saw his films I could not really make a distinction between documentary and fiction; I was just touched by the characters. None of the actors were known to me, so it could well have been documentary. When I started producing my own films I used everything to make a point; professional actors and everyday people. Many people found my early films problematic—*Homage*, which I shot on my own, was based on everyday life in my village and featured the funeral of my father, who had died whilst I was still at university here in France. At the time of his death I didn't have the means to go back. I had to work for a year to earn enough to return home. When eventually I did go, I took an Arri ST camera and a small tape recorder. Since I had no sync-sound, I had to make a shot and then take the sound. After shooting four rolls the camera broke down, but I had a small Leica so I carried on with stills only. It was the '80s and, to my mind, people generally found documentaries boring, so I thought why not make reality as entertaining as a feature film? I wrote a long commentary describing what I felt at that time, but that proved too long and dull. By turning it into a conversation between two imaginary people—one who had left the village, and the other who stayed— I managed to make it more lively. I asked two friends who were actors to read the conversation, and I recorded it in my small room at home. *Homage* is a very personal film. It was a kind of therapy for me because I had to wait so long to attend my father's funeral. It was like finishing, turning a page of my life. It doesn't look like a feature film and you can't say it is a documentary. I attribute the approach to the influence of Ken Loach. I don't know what happened, but someone decided to show the film at the Nyon film festival one year, and it won a prize. Then at the Cinéma du Réel festival it won the short-film prize. And that's really how this small film that I made alone started going around the world and became my first major work.

I am not concerned with fashion or trend; I just want to find the most effective way to express things that matter to me. I make films in the hope of revealing a situation in my country to the rest of the world, and maybe to help bring about some change. I hate to speak and say nothing, so when I speak I want to be able to say something worthwhile. Making films for me was a way to get around the censorship that exists in my country. Many journalists have had serious problems. I remember a film made by a Cameroon filmmaker, dealing with the issue of the dowry, which could be quite prohibitive for the person paying it. It was a comedy and so popular that the government enforced a limit on the size of a dowry. I was so impressed by the fact that a film could affect such

*Homage*, 1985

changes in society that I thought, this is how to get around censorship and to speak about things government don't want to talk about. So my need to make films stemmed from the fact that I really wanted to talk about the neighborhood where I grew up, and to talk about the situation of my people who could not speak for themselves.

I shoot myself, but the editing I don't do, although I edited for television. I was lucky to have an editor friend who cut my first film, and since then I have never really edited any of my work. I need to have a bit of distance from what I shoot because I make films to talk to people, and I need to make sure that I'm not talking only to myself. I always want an editor who can look at things and tell me if it makes sense or not. Now I work more and more with Christiane Badgley, my wife, who is a documentary director and editor. It's not easy working with someone so close to you personally. It can affect both your private relationship and the edit. When it works, it works very well, but when there is misunderstanding, everything suffers. Finding an editor with whom you can establish a long-term relationship is not easy.

I made my first film with my own money—I didn't know anything about the process of financing. Then I met filmmakers who told me, "You shouldn't be doing that, you should find a producer." But French producers were not interested in my vision of Africa, and I was not interested in making documentaries about African drums and dances. So I had to produce and distribute my own work. I took short courses on scriptwriting and film funding, and gradually I began to understand how the system works. Now I even produce for other directors, and do all the distribution of my own films.

Europeans have had a tendency to monopolize certain aspects of life. Yes, we live in a world of interaction where people and products are constantly traveling. The first films I saw back home were Indian, American, and French. I came to Europe to get away from Africa; and only then did I really start to learn about my own history. Now I know even more about African history than if I'd stayed in the Cameroon. The whole system is based on colonization and keeping people dependent, so we learn just a small amount about European culture and none about our own. I have access to vast sources of information, I'm free to question things, and free to move. I'm free to make films that speak for what I really stand for; to challenge things that I don't like in my own society, and by doing that to challenge the attitude of people here towards Africa. I question how it is that people accept being under dictatorship. The 16th-century writer Étienne De La Boétie wrote in Discours de la Servitude Volontaire that for every tyrant above there are many lesser tyrants below who oppress the people and, in turn, the people will find those that they can oppress. By oppressing others, one accepts being oppressed. Well, I reached the conclusion that Cameroon lives in a kind of "*servitude volontaire*." There is always a father or king figure that holds the power—everyone wants a little bit for themselves so as to oppress others, and so on, until the number of those unhappy with the system becomes greater than those who benefit from it. That's going to be very hard to change.

With the growing popularity of the video camera everyone is a potential documentary maker. You just need to have some experience of life. I myself started quite late on. The more I make film, the more

I like simplicity in structure and story. *Alex's Wedding*, which I shot in 1999, was very simple. An event that ran from noon until one in the morning, very linear, and yet to make it interesting was anything but simple. Finding a rhythm within a story which is essentially just one event is more difficult than interweaving a number of events. A neighbor in my village was to marry—this was to be his second wife. In my village tradition, the first wife must be at the marriage, and should appear to be happy about it. This guy was in his early forties, his first wife in her mid-thirties, and the second wife was in her early twenties. The first wife went through with the charade, but I could see she was so sad. I shot a three-hour tape and realized, when putting it together, that this could be more than just a wedding video. I hadn't wanted to make a sociological study of polygamy, but the moment when the two young women started living together was very interesting. The older of the two wives asked the other why she had cried when leaving her family home—after all, she didn't have to get married —as she had the choice of refusing to move into the house. And the younger woman replied, "It's my life insurance, being married is my life insurance." You see, the system only continues because some women are ready to accept it. Even more disturbing is that the first woman must have suffered that day as the new wife moved in, but she'll forget as she too will push her son to find a second wife, because when a son has only one wife the mother is no longer dominant. But with more than one wife the mother restores her position of importance in the family. I made *Alex's Wedding* for women who have forgotten their suffering and sorrow. Approaching polygamy from this angle has never really been done; the attitude has always been, "OK, it's tradition or it's Islam."

*Bikutsi Water Blues*, 1988

*Bikutsi Water Blues*, 1988

Top: *Chief!*, 1999

Above: *A Trip to the Country*, 2000

*Africa, I Will Fleece You*, 1992

*Bikutsi Water Blues*, 1988

*Chief!* could only have been made on video. In 1997 I was back home when I came across a 16-year-old boy who had stolen a chicken and four chicks. The boy was about to be lynched by a mob. I'd seen on television a few days before that when a thief is caught, people will often just beat him to death. Anyway, the violence around this young boy was building up, and I decided to shoot using my old DSR200. Although I had dealt with violence before, I was now seeing it for the first time in close-up, and witnessing the escalating hysteria of the mob. At one point I intervened—I couldn't just stand there filming the boy being beaten to death! That same week a journalist friend of mine had been arrested because he asked a question in his newspaper about the head of state having had a heart attack during a football match. My friend spent the next ten months in jail. These two, apparently unconnected, events happened almost at the same moment and made me consider the whole issue of servitude and prejudice in my country.

Then I discovered, printed on the back of an exercise book, a set of rules and regulations for women and wives, such as, "The man is always the head of the family," or "A woman in bed with her husband must ask permission to turn her back on him." I asked my cousins about these things and they said, "Yes, that is what they tell people when they get married." I said, "No, that's not possible." And they told me to ask the mayor's office, and said, "Very probably they'll give you all the same regulations." Of course, it was not true; the laws are the same as those in France. But this attitude is so deeply rooted in people's minds that this form of oppression of women is commonly regarded as official. Gradually *Chief!* evolved, but without a video camera I would not have been able to follow either event. I shot the boy and the mob for almost an hour non-stop. This was a film that just developed as it happened. That is what video

allows; the ability to react to the unexpected. Yet it took me nearly nine months to finish, because I really didn't know where I was going. When I started, all I knew was that this poor kid was a thief and from the mood of the crowd it was obvious that there was going to be a lynching. What was interesting for me was the whole process leading up to a lynching. Usually what you see on television is just a corpse and nothing of how the mob got so excited and reached that point of no return. I said to myself, if they want to go that far I'm going to be here with a camera to record it. They asked me if I was from the national news. I told them, "No, I'm like a reporter from an opposition newspaper." So they left me alone, and I went on filming. One old man was saying not to beat him, to take him to the police. Others were saying, "No, a thief must die." They started hitting him, and I heard the sound of a heavy thud in the speaker of the camera. That was the point at which I stopped and positioned myself between the boy and the mob. These guys were 18- and 20-year-olds, and I was over 40, but I thought, if they want to lynch a thief they're not going to attack me just because I told them to stop. Eventually they calmed down and someone said, "OK, we're going to take him to the *chef du quartier.*"

Each project dictates its own essentials. For some I shoot film, and others I might mix 16mm with interviews in video, as I did for *A Trip to the Country.* The 16mm was for all the scenes establishing location, while the video camera allowed me to gain proximity and talk to people. Post-production was in video and then I made a tape-to-35mm transfer. With my own video camera and editing equipment, budgets become easier to handle. The television companies in France are not really interested in my projects, so I've developed a strategy to distribute my documentaries directly into cinemas. Some of my films have never been on television, even though I have had good press reviews and

journalists have complained that my films weren't shown. We send material to the television companies all the time, but they ignore us. At school we were taught "*liberté, égalité, fraternité,*" but even for the blacks, even the French-born blacks from the suburbs of Paris, Lyon, or Marseilles, filmmakers or otherwise, it's impossible to access the television channels. Television executives say they want stories about life in the *banlieues* of France, but they only want to see through the eyes of their own directors, people just like them from white, bourgeois, or privileged backgrounds. So a black documentary maker from the suburbs who wants to talk about his neighborhood has no chance, he's not going to portray what the rest of the society wants to see. Sometimes social prejudices can be alleviated, but racial ones are never talked about. The French don't want to talk about their colonial history, so how can they deal with racial conflict?

I don't claim any objectivity at all. When I start a film I always try to say here I am, Jean-Marie Teno, and my background is this… I'm telling you the story from this point of view… is what is shown on television objective? Or is it not just a way to manipulate? Objectivity seems to be the reserve of those who hold power; their opinions are always "objective," whereas those who oppose are considered subjective. I film situations from my "subjective" point of view, and in Cameroon none of my films get shown on television. So I say to the young filmmaker who asks, "Jean-Marie, how do I get going?" that there is nothing more important than to be yourself—struggle, fight, and learn, but be yourself.

# Paul
# Watson

### An introduction

A streetwise youngster, Watson learnt the way of the world in London before his family moved to Lancashire and a grammar school that taught him "how to learn and ask questions." He was to have become a painter and entered the Royal College of Art along with David Hockney, only to realize that his true medium was film, with which he could layer words and music, light and shade, movement and storytelling. His career has taken him to the BBC, Channel Four, and ITV, where he produced and directed many highly original and innovative documentaries, such as *The Family*, *The Fishing Party*, which attracted much criticism from former Prime Minister Thatcher, *Sylvania Waters, The Dinner Party*, and in 2002, *The Queen's Wedding*.

# Paul Watson

*Tonbridge, April 11 and 17, 2002*

I was a leader of a gang of thieves until the age of ten. Then I got nicked giving money to my friends. We lived in North London in two rooms, with another part of our family. I got into more trouble, and we moved to Bolton in Lancashire, with a Mrs Riding, who kept pigeons. I'd be in prison now if I hadn't gone to a grammar school. They taught me how to learn, think, and ask questions. By the end I was doing 27 out of 35 lessons a week in the art room. The headmaster wasn't pleased—but I was, unknowingly, on the road to making documentaries.

At the Royal College of Art, led by David Hockney and others I was painting pop art, not decorative but political. I have a drawing in the national collection which is an early exploration of the problems of Yugoslavia. I was involved in trying to understand injustice, and painting was the wrong medium. When I found filmmaking it was like finding opera. I was a painter who discovered that words and music, motion and time, were more exciting than putting paint on canvas. In those days we thought of film as a means, a tool to better understand the realities of what was going on in the country. In the '60s we looked at the status quo and said, "It's bollocks." But in painting, fashion, and film, things were starting to happen. I saw very few films and there's no director that I feel influences me, although I do have an enormous regard for Peter Watkins. I think he's a difficult bugger, and I recognize elements of him in me. He was braver, probably more talented, and more bloody-minded even than me. Then James Cameron, a man to learn from even when drunk. It was his ability to understand the human condition that made him an exceptional journalist and taught me how to translate observation.

The first thing I saw on television was the Queen's coronation in 1953. I was always getting told off for not doing the washing up because I was sneaking off to watch television. It was, for a while, a way to express yourself. But the television industry no longer wants personal expression with a real sense of social purpose. Today I am something of a dinosaur.

Our lives are made up of trivia. In *The Family*, Mrs Wilkins is seen in the kitchen of her crowded flat coping on a low income, managing her growing children, peeling potatoes, and arguing. When I told the BBC I wanted to make a film about a family "just living," I think they expected I'd chuck out the nose-picking and the love-making. I did. But today picking the nose would be kept, simply because that's meant to be good television—"Oh, you've got him picking his nose and crying. Marvelous!" Some people at the BBC thought there could be big issues in *The Family* and that I'd cut the trivia and keep the, "How do you live on 30 shillings a week?" stuff. They thought, "factual broadcasting"—I didn't. I wanted the personal and the idiosyncratic. We got letters from pompous, middle-class people complaining *The Family* had nothing to offer; that it was a gimmick, and I was using people. Ten years later the series was repeated, and we received many letters saying, "When Margaret did such-and-such with her child, I complained, I never thought I would do that to my child. But having done the same myself, I just want to apologize for the letter I wrote ten years ago." Now that's the privilege of making films which can influence.

Documentaries exist because people are naturally nosey. Walk down a street, the curtains are open—you look in. Hear a ding-dong next door—you listen. If you turn it into something creative and useful we might better understand why a parent slapped their kid around the head. Why one reaction was so negative or so positive. We British don't talk to each other much, so *The Family* was a sort of ersatz conversation for ordinary people. People talk to me about anything and everything. Afterwards they feel something has been lanced, a small boil of anger, dismay, frustration, a sense of pride exhaustively revealed. They say, "At least he bloody listened, at least he bloody wanted to know." People still think that if you're from "the television" you're somehow part of government, some sort of authority.

Marian Wilkins and Tom
Bernes' wedding
*The Family*, 1974

The Wilkins
*The Family*, 1974

Marion Wilkins and fiancé Tom Bernes
*The Family*, 1974

Cas Mathee, champion pigeon breeder
*White Lives*, 1998

*The Factory* was a film about life in a factory. I had asked the cameraman to get some close-ups of women's faces and their hands going in and out of the machinery, just missing having their fingers cut off by eighths of an inch, doing this day in, day out, tired or not—you know, worrying about their old men at home on the dole. I had to go off to sort something out with the foreman. When I returned I saw four bored film-crew—my eyes, ears, brain, soul, my representatives—desperate for their cup of tea, desperate to talk about their company shares, or whatever—awful. I thought, this is all so old-fashioned; there's got to be a better way to get inside people without this baggage and me being their manager. So I looked at the new technology.

For the fifth anniversary of South African black rule I made *White Lives*. I went with a brilliant film cameraman, but I also took a Sony VX1000. I used it to film gangsters and kids who were murderers, and all sorts of other things that might put my crew in danger. The crew got a bit pissed off, not that they wanted to film the dangerous stuff, they just felt that they were the photographers, and what did I know? Well, Mr Sony is a brilliant photographer, and if you read the camera manual you can learn how to get the focus and exposure correct. Politicians, and others, thought the little camera a bit Mickey Mouse. But it enabled me to gather hard-to-obtain interviews.

I resolved to shoot the next film on my own. With the experience of *White Lives* (three hours), the vast majority of which looked wonderful, I got interviews with young gangsters who would not have talked to a bored camera crew. They talked to me because I was genuinely interested to understand how a person could walk up to a car with a gun hidden in a bunch of flowers and just shoot someone in the head. This story was told in an uncuttable, 16-minute take, by a young gang member. Just him and me in a room with a small camera. Intimacy.

Prior to *White Lives* I went to Channel Four with an idea about racism in the East End of London. I spent £10,000 of the commissioning editor's money and then went back and said, "I screwed up, the film isn't there. At least not what I thought was there."

I couldn't face the messages that were coming out. The BBC's soap, *EastEnders*, was lionizing the Cockney spirit, and I wanted to find what it was that made a Cockney. In the end I liked the Pakistanis so much more than the whites. They said, "We're poor, but we're making a life. It's better than what it was, and it'll get better tomorrow." Then, I found myself sitting in a caravan talking to a white racist pig who kept hitting the greasy table. A voice in me said, "When he hits that bloody table again, that's it—I'm going to go back to Channel Four to tell them it's too unpalatable a message." Not that it wouldn't have got them an audience, it's just that I don't think I could have done it—I was so angry and upset.

*Malcolm and Barbara: A Love Story* was going to take however long Malcolm at 52 years old with Alzheimer's had left to live (four years). Barbara, his wife, agreed to my filming on the understanding that I would be there at the end. As you can't get a crew at a day's notice, I decided to shoot it myself. I think the material is more spare, more direct, not a lot of charging around, gung-ho-like camera work. When you're trying to pull focus and be intimate with your questioning, it is better to let the camera determine the style.

*The Queen's Wedding*, a film about gay men, I also shot on video with a single assistant. Once they had worked out that I wasn't some heterosexual looking for a new sex kick they told me things that, they said, "I'd never 'av told me mother." While we were in Manchester we telephoned a pub, searching for people to take part in the film. I heard a booming voice ask the pub, "Anybody want to talk about fucking poofs?..." The voice came down the telephone line, "Yeah, you'd better come down luv, they all want to talk." In the pub, the most horrendous homophobic things were said in ignorance. I left feeling very sad; these men were very unhappy, in rotten relationships with their wives, most were on the scrap heap at 50 years old, with no pride in anything. There was nothing erotic in the content of *The Queen's Wedding*. Maybe there should have been. Sure there would have been a bit of pixelation, but the film would have got more viewers. I'm not gay, I just wanted to make a film about men who wore women's clothes.

It's passion that drives the creative force, the mind and soul unite, and you become a menace to live with. I have had a terrible time with relationships in my private life because I'm obsessed by making films about other people, and trying to get into their psyche. That's the way I live, that's what I do, and it's very old-fashioned. When not making films I make tapestries and weave lots of images, but I'd never edit a film because you can fall so in love with the technique, with the medium, that you lose the point of the story. So I dry rent the edit kit and work in my home with an editor. I never say, "Here's the rushes, I'm off to the South of France, when I come back can I see a rough cut?" I'm here every day and I'm a pain, because I'm constantly trying to tell a familiar story in a refreshed form, triple-layering, triple-parallel-action, and it's the hardest thing to bring off, but when you do it's fantastic; it's like great sex or great pecan pies. Every now and then you go vrooom. But when the form goes wrong, it's the editor who gets me out of the cutting room and out of trouble. So the editor is a sounding board and yes, I pick people who respect my left-of-field view on life. Professionals, artists in their own right. They come on Monday morning and leave on Friday evening. We get 12 hours a day done, sometimes 16. There's one rule—I make dinner and we don't talk about the film over the meal. It's fantastic. I don't make films from A to Z—I might start in the middle, put in a little of this and a little of that. Yes, with a beginning, middle, and end, but as Godard would say, "not necessarily in that order."

Britain is a country where, "Is he one of us?" still applies. You're an outsider if you're not an insider. Our country and way of living are not questioned enough. I'm a subversive, but I don't wish to overturn the state, only to question, to view things from a different perspective. I don't say, "There is only one right way." Perhaps because television is controlled by so few people we've got used to there being only one acceptable view. With *The Fishing Party* I thought, here we go, a group of toffs who want me to make a holiday video about them. I was about to tell my boss to find someone else—fortunately I didn't. I asked him what they did. "I don't know, something in the City of London." For some time I had been trying to make a film about

*The Queen's Wedding*, 2002

corporate fat cats and the lie they sell about how relevant and necessary they are. So we met and went drinking in champagne bars of the City for about five days before shooting began. The program is still shown around the world as a way to make political films that don't have a single politician in them. By careful juxtaposition, I reinterpret that which appears as "everyday" to other people. Hydrogen and oxygen are very ordinary gases, put them together and something is revealed—the hidden context, "a drop of water." I've made other, better films, but *The Fishing Party* still has its worth—it is former Prime Minister Margaret Thatcher's least favorite film—and the BBC received a huge number of complaints. Sometime later, after about six episodes of *Sylvania Waters,* which I made in Australia, I was kicked out of the BBC. My boss said the films were not politically correct and I could no longer be trusted. Shame, because it was about real people; there is no point in my turning my subjects into people they're not, as I might just as well make drama.

I wake up with a line, a simple idea, like those in the television listings that trigger audience interest. If I can't hold them after that then I'm stuffed, probably because I'm not good enough. I get an idea, usually a cliché, then I set out to debunk it, confirm it, whatever. As I dig deeper and pass from person to person within the subject area, I formulate a deeper insight but only in my mind, I don't put anything together in terms of sequences or shooting. When I do start, I shoot things which seem intriguing, appalling, informative, celebratory, but I haven't a clue where they're going in the film, nor if it's going to get in at all. I can't even tell a commissioning editor the opening sequence. John Birt, ex-director general of the BBC, who in my opinion probably did as much harm to television as Thatcher, issued a dictat that you should have the opening sequence and the raison d'être and the conclusions of the film before starting. If that's what's needed, write a play!

There is so much celebrity stuff which purports to be serious documentary. A lot of it is Hello! magazine produced by an agent. It's not about that wonderful thing that happens when you get different groups of people rubbing against each other. But defining "documentary" is pointless; the language of definition is so incredibly confused. For example, I thought I made "reality television," but it turns out that reality television is constructed realism. *Big Brother* is called "reality television," but it couldn't be further from reality.

Contemporary fashion does not want to know about the social ills in our communities, not in any meaningful depth. I was rung up by a young producer and asked if I'd like to make a film about men trying to go straight. "Never been done before," she said. Now I've made that film twice. So I asked, "How many people are you thinking of following?" "Oh, about nine." And I said, "Would you do me a favor and just follow one, or possibly two, because you know there's the depth that you have to get into, there's the boredom, and the pressures pulling them back into the mire." And this woman said to me, "That's why we asked you, because you are so good at boring subjects." It's true, I do make films about watching paint dry, but I think it's riveting. When people say to me, "I love documentaries," I know they mean animals, jungles, fish, and so on—that's not what documentaries are for. The documentary should be about understanding people and the human conundrum. But that's unfashionable and unwanted.

*Sylvania Waters,* 1992

Noeline Baker and Laurie Donaher
*Sylvania Waters*, 1992

# Interview
# Wu
# Wenguang

# 13

## An introduction

The first of very few—Wu Wenguang was China's
first "independent" documentary maker. He has
won a place among the world's most respected
directors, with films shown at festivals
on three continents. His childhood was dominated
by the events of the Cultural Revolution. After
graduating from Yünnan University in 1982,
Wenguang taught for three years before entering
television as a news journalist. He left in 1989 to
become *the* independent documentary
filmmaker in China. Since 1994, he has
written, acted, and produced for the theater
and co-operated with Chinese experimental
theater/dance. In 2001 Wenguang founded the
independent art monthly magazine Next Wave, as
well as courses in media and journalism at Beijing
University. Wenguang was a jury member at
the Singapore International Film Festival, and
is to be on the juries of the Berlin Film Festival
and the Visions du Réel in Nyon, Switzerland.

# Wu Wenguang

*Beijing, September 13, 2002*

I was born in 1956 in the Yünnan Province in China. During the Cultural Revolution that followed, my father was sent away for 13 years to be re-educated. All my family was dispatched to various parts of China during that time. I, too, was sent to the countryside for four years, as was my sister. At the age of 79, my father returned. We were told my father had "problems," so at first I didn't feel sad about his absence. I truly believed the Party was right and, like others, I wanted to follow their ideology. I hated my father and felt shame for what I thought he had brought on our family. I went willingly to the countryside. Then in 1978 I went to university to study Chinese, and not until 1979 did the whole family get reunited.

I became a documentary maker after the era of Chairman Mao and the Cultural Revolution. In the years following 1978, me and fellow students and workers started to have doubts about blindly following the Party's ideology. I wanted to express my own ideas, to think in a free way. By "free" I don't mean I wished to follow Western ideas, because that too is an ideology; rather that I just wanted to follow what I thought was right. China changed after 1978, from being a closed society to a gradually opening one. I began to read the work of Heidegger, Sartre, Rousseau and others that expressed these free ideas; that is where my major inspiration for my documentaries came from. Like a hungry child, I read a great deal in a short time.

I started to write poetry, which I still do, as well as short stories and a long novel, which charts my development since the Cultural Revolution as I gradually made the transition from "collectivist" to "individualist," which took nearly ten years. After graduation from university in 1982 I was assigned to a secondary school to teach Chinese. I didn't choose that work, however, and after three years

I managed to find a job in a television station as a journalist, producing propaganda advertisements. I found that very boring, so in 1988 I moved to Beijing and joined China Central Television (CCTV) on a program celebrating the 40th anniversary of the Chinese Republic. The program was similar to a documentary. In the period prior to the Tiananmen Square incident, China was quite open; there was freedom, and so we tried to make something worthwhile, not just propaganda. Actually, the whole of Chinese society before Tiananmen Square was very heavily influenced by Western democratic ideas of freedom. We didn't have it, though—we just tried to have it.

To understand why I became a documentary filmmaker it is important to recognize that Tiananmen Square, in 1989, was a watershed in our history. Like many others, I felt excited by the prospect of more freedom. Many people took to the streets, I, too, went to the Square, but the whole world knows about that day already. I started to develop a new way of thinking; as China was not ready to adopt Western notions of freedom, I had to follow my own convictions and become an independent. Some friends went to France, England and the USA to study. I, too, applied to go. As my friends were leaving China, I thought it would be interesting to produce something about their departure. I wasn't sure it was a documentary, but I started to shoot anyway. At once I came to the realization that this was what I really wanted to do in life. I had no money for the production, so together with a friend who worked in cinema, we borrowed a Betacam from CCTV. Although I knew how to use the camera I didn't know anything about documentary—I hadn't seen any documentaries yet at that time. It was only in 1991 that I started seeing them at international film festivals.

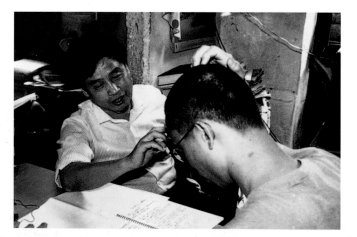

Right: Wu Wenguang (right) with an old Red Guard
*1966, My Time in the Red Guards,*
1992 Far right: Tian Zhuangzhuang, another ex-Red Guard
*1966, My Time in the Red Guards,* 1992

*Life on the Road*, 1999

At CCTV, we were encouraged to handle subjects in a clear and straightforward manner, so of course, when I made my own film, I made it without music or voiceover. I'd rather use very simple captions relating to places, people, and even a summary or brief explanation of events—I never use commentary. It was very satisfying to produce something entirely for myself without having to be restricted by the sensitivities of CCTV. In order to earn a living, however, I had to continue working at the station.

Then in 1992 I began working on a documentary called *1966, My Time in the Red Guards*, in which I explored my feelings about the Cultural Revolution. I also wrote a book that, together with the documentary, reflected my positive feelings towards it. In 1994 I started *At Home in the World*, a continuation of *Bumming in Beijing* (my first documentary, which I started to shoot in 1988, and finished in 1990), with the same five characters that were in the first film. Every five years I visited these people to record how their lives had changed. They are all now living in Europe and the USA. As I couldn't get any sponsors in China, I looked for overseas finance. A Chinese friend in Tokyo invested, and I also received some funding from an arts festival. So it was that I became the first "independent" documentary maker in China. Now there are a few other independents in documentary, and even one in feature films.

Other than free showings in bars, universities, or libraries and those kinds of public places, my documentaries have never been seen on television or in the cinema in China. Not that my work is regarded as politically unacceptable, rather that my films are quite independently produced and the cinemas and television belong to the state. It is very difficult for independents to get permission to show their work in the government-controlled media. The public are not really interested in films that are longer than 30 minutes anyway; if they want documentaries at all, they want short, easily understood popular films. However, since 1999 more and more young people want to produce documentaries, experimental movies, and shorts. Some try to organize screenings and are looking for places to present their work and, in fact, we have found some suitable venues in Beijing.

Prior to 1999 I knew my work would not be broadcast in mainland China, so I never even submitted it to the television service. But in that year an editor from the Beijing studios, who knew that I was filming *Life on the Road*, asked me whether I would let his studio broadcast it. However, the head of that studio turned down his proposal, saying that the documentary did not give the audience a sense of a bright future in China. Now I am in post-production on my sixth documentary. I made my previous films on video with a small crew, but on the last two I have worked with just an assistant, using either a Sony PD150 or a Sony 110 camera, and I do all the post-production myself at home with Premiere 6.0 edit software. I have given up using big cameras (like the Betacam) and a full editing suite so as to work alone. In this way I've found the freedom to work like a freelance writer, and that makes me extremely happy.

When I begin filming, I don't normally think too much about my approach. The main topic of interest usually emerges during shooting and in the process of adding more people and more events to the film. When I feel all the material I have could

*Dance with the Farm Workers*, 2001

form a meaningful documentary, I say to myself, "OK, it's time to edit," and I do this myself. My way of working enables me to afford a year to make, for example, *Life on the Road*. The title is a popular phrase that means, "those who live outside the system." The film follows a group of traveling performers working in rural China. After a week or two they totally accepted me and were completely oblivious of the camera. I lived with them for a few months. I don't like to write a script, as I prefer to just observe reality. I sat among them and filmed as one of them—just a person with a small camera. In China, if people spend time thinking and talking together it is easy to develop good relationships, because you are seen as a friend, especially after getting drunk together. On one occasion, during a performance, they had a problem with the people of the local village. There was a disturbance and a fight. The police intervened and I tried to find a way to solve their differences, which made it impossible to carry on shooting. I became completely involved, because by then they were my friends. When all was resolved we did plenty of laughing, talking, and, of course, drinking. I don't believe in objectivity—the first and most important thing is to develop relationships.

If you are dealing with real people and their life stories, it is almost inevitable that issues over privacy will arise. The way I handle it is that if the person I am shooting requests not to be filmed I will, of course, comply. And if I know the content may cause others a problem, I will cut it as well. Unfortunately, sometimes an undesirable effect won't turn up until the film is shown.

Normally there are stories in my movies; although *Life on the Road* is about one group of performers, there are small stories within it. I am interested in people who, for one reason or another, are forced to abandon their position. I like to reflect in my films their desire to pursue their dreams; some go abroad, others stay to realize their dreams, be it the arts or making money. So far, my films have had this in common. I am very happy with the situation I am in and what I am doing here in China. I am not too old, only 46, so I wonder what the future holds for me? I have seen big changes during my life, like the Cultural Revolution and Tiananmen Square. OK, of course, I have a lot of constraints placed on me in China, but my future is certainly here.

To be honest, I don't think I have achieved anything in documentary filmmaking yet. What I have done so far is just to do what I want to do. But regarding personal achievement, I would say that I have gradually built up my own style and independent thinking during these ten years of documentary shooting and editing. That is what I am most proud of. So at the moment, all I want to do is make one film after another. However, my own preferred documentary style is not always popular with others, nor even commercially viable. I have just come back from Laos where I organized a video workshop for ten-year-old children. Maybe I will go back there to film some documentaries related to the people of Laos, because I really enjoyed my time there and the people as well. Last year I visited some ethnic groups in the Yünnan Province where I was born. I shot some material for research purposes, but so far, I haven't decided what to do with it yet.

I see a big problem ahead now. After 1997 more and more young people began to make documentaries. The availability of small digital cameras in China has made it easier for them to become filmmakers. I now see quite a few new films each year: six or even eight—whereas before 1997 there would be maybe one a year or even every two years. So I believe this new technology is a big opportunity for the documentary maker. But I don't think the documentary will ever be big business. However, nobody now can stop young people from making documentary films. I'm not sure about what the future of documentary film will be in this country, because the present situation makes it so difficult to say. It seems we are just at the beginning, and I believe there is hope.

I have just written an article entitled Just on the Road, in which I go over what was happening during the '90s. I wanted to reflect on the way I looked at the process of making documentary at that time—my own perspective. At the beginning, I was not clear about ideas like independence and democracy. In the article, I wrote that even now I am not sure about the real meaning of independence for documentary making in China. When I started making documentary films, I realized that I was not really free to work in the way I wanted while working at CCTV. So I decided to become an independent and make something for myself, and actually I then managed to make better films. During the '90s it went really well. In those years more and more people in China started looking at ways to make money, including some involved in documentary film. They opened companies to work for the television broadcasters. But I feel that if television is the only source of income for the so-called independent, then we don't have a real understanding of the word "independence." This is just a start; we are trying to learn what it is to be independent as we didn't make the transition to it through any real freedom. So we could say we are just on the road. I have the feeling that most young people are only trying to make films so as to become famous, and they want, in particular, to become successful on the international circuit. Their work is of a different nature to mine; they want to achieve quickly, and are not willing to take a long-term approach.

So I don't know what will happen in this field. What I do know is that the documentary changed my life. I could never have been an artist in fiction, inventing a story. I don't like dramatization, and as for reconstruction, I have never used it before, but am just starting to. I don't know enough about it to comment at this stage. I have always looked at the reality of my life, of the situations I found myself in. It is difficult to express, but the documentary is real life for me, and in the process of making documentaries I feel that I am facing real life, and in this way I do not try to avoid it, I do not try to escape it, and that makes me braver—this is very important. I am the person I am through this experience.

*Bumming in Beijing: The Last Dreamers*,
1990

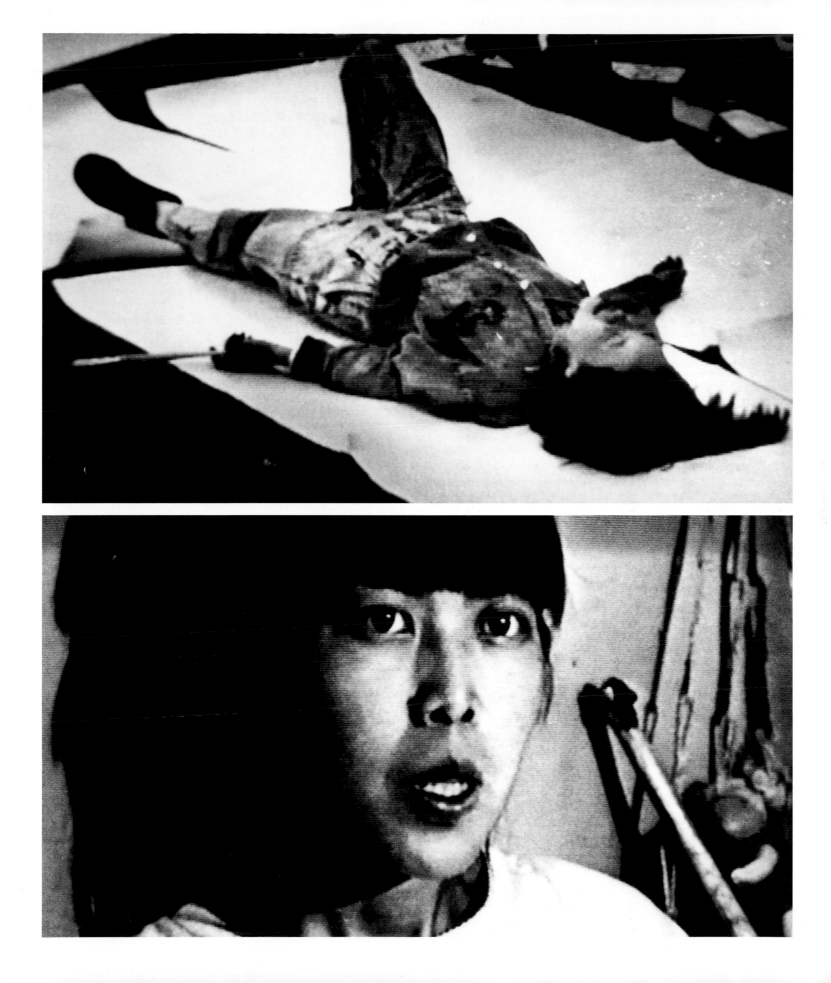

# Interview
# John Willis

14

## An introduction

Truly the offspring of television, his father was a successful television scriptwriter. Willis took a postgraduate year under the distinguished George Brand at Bristol University in England, before finding his way into television, and then there was no holding him back. At Yorkshire Television he moved quickly through the documentary department to become the leading investigative documentary maker in Britain. Willis went on to Channel Four as controller of factual programs, moving up to director of programs in 1993. Four years later, he became chief executive of United Productions, then managing director of London Weekend Television and United Productions, before becoming managing director of worldwide production at Granada Content in 2001. In the summer of 2002, in his latest challenge, he moved to the Public Broadcasting Service (PBS) in the USA. His son and daughter are both finding their way in British television—the apple doesn't fall far.

# John Willis

*Tonbridge, April 11, 2002*

I'm a child of television. My father wrote *Dixon of Dock Green*, the very popular police series of the '60s. Until I went into television I didn't realize how much I'd learnt by a process of osmosis. I ran the film society at a school in south-east London. One of my colleagues made a documentary called *Suburban Sunday*, which I edited on a bit of equipment I had. Of course, the film was as boring as a suburban Sunday, but I got addicted to film. After studying history at Cambridge, I did a postgraduate year at Bristol on a radio, film, and television course, which was fairly experimental in those days (1969 to 1970). The first week we did a radio exercise. I was very under-confident, and thought, "These people are cleverer than me. I'm not sure I'm any good at this stuff." George Brand, the lecturer, got excited about my exercise, and I realized perhaps I had a modicum of talent. Brand was very inspiring in the sense that he set high intellectual benchmarks for what television and film could achieve. After that, a friend who was the road manager for the band Thunderclap Newman told me that no one could afford to pay for a "video" of their first record, Something in the Air. I raised £75 and directed a three-minute film of the song. The song got to number one and our film was used in several countries. And that was how I got started in the industry.

Most of my films were made at a time when advertising revenue seemed to fall off trees. Management was in the hands of people committed to programs, people who had come up through programs; journalists, program editors, and documentary makers. Today, management tend to be business people and accountants who don't share quite the same values. Those running commercial television in the '60s, '70s, and the first few years of the '80s, knew that the business had a set of values that underpinned it. Commercial television believed it had to make some serious documentaries as well as making entertainment and drama. I was a part of that commitment. Today, in the UK, the commissioning process is a daunting experience. The eye of the needle has got smaller, and the power of channel controllers greater. Young program makers find it tough. Funding is difficult, and you need to have a strong relationship with a

commissioner who can act as your patron and mentor to encourage, nurture, and push you through, and there's not many of those about.

Film has a kind of creative and intellectual discipline. In my day documentaries were all on film. Now it's great not to worry about how many rolls of film you use, but with video, which costs less, you can shoot everything that moves. And the danger is not to think about what you want out of a sequence, or what it really means. But clearly the intimacy of small video cameras is something I look on with envy, because the television documentary is good at the small story, the intimate, the domestic, and the familial. There is something about seeing life reflected back at you within the privacy of your home. Documentary is a journey of discovery on which you take the audience and show them what you've experienced, and what you think is important. You've got to be flexible enough to throw questions away, start again, use interviews in a different way. What was said may not have been expected, but it is valuable. The interview is one of the cornerstones of the documentary. When filming, I carefully thought out the pattern of questions and knew where a particular interview would fit in, what overall contribution it might make. I tried to build a relationship with interviewees. I've formed personal bonds with the central figures, so that the interview became a conversation. They might have frustrations or difficulties, but I helped them to explore and explain their views of the world through interviews that were intimate and open. The documentaries I made were research intensive, so I was lucky in having researchers like James Cutler and Peter Moore, two of the best. But the cameramen and editors contributed hugely—I often worked with the same people.

I can't think of many examples where I've paid fees to interviewees; sometimes they took a day off work, so I paid some expenses, took them out for lunch. But when people give evidence about a crime, a misdemeanor, or a social ill, I think it's inadvisable to pay, because the film can finish up in a court case. Quite a lot of documentaries I made did end up in those circumstances where the press, the government, committees of enquiry, or the

*The Case of Yolande McShane*, 1978

*Johnny Go Home*, 1976

Roger Gleaves (left), the "Bishop of
Medway," and Johnny
*Johnny Go Home*, 1976

regulators, went through the films with a fine toothcomb. When an interviewee said, "I worked in a mental hospital and I saw someone beaten up," I needed to be careful not to have paid for the interview, otherwise the evidence could be undermined. I think it's different when it's more of a social documentary. People explaining their personal situation in terms of, for example, asbestos-related illness or running away from home, will tell you that story, whether you pay them or not. And I found it difficult to be working with kids on the streets when, after filming, you and the crew go home or to an hotel and they are left to sleep in a doorway—now, how do you reconcile that in terms of payment? It's not easy.

"Trial by television" or "invasion of privacy" are labels often used to describe documentaries that are critical or expose someone. The guardians of television get very concerned about issues of privacy. It's a matter of balancing privacy against public interest. I'm convinced the documentaries I made were very much in the public interest. Exposing assaults in a mental hospital, such as in *Rampton—The Secret Hospital*, is certainly in the public interest. Or the scandal of runaway kids who finish up in London, where neither local authorities nor government provide for them, and the best society has to offer are rundown private hostels, as in *Johnny Go Home*—that too was in the public interest.

One of the things that makes documentaries interesting is surprise. You have to follow your instincts, change direction and meaning, even when filming. For example, the main protagonist in the investigative part of *Johnny Go Home* was Roger Gleaves, who called himself the Bishop of Medway. He was a man who picked up young people who had run away from home in Scotland or the North of England, and arrived at central London railway stations without anywhere to go. He befriended them and took them to hostels he ran. Gleaves looked respectable, appearing to do a good job at the rough end of society. We started filming in a hostel and one or two of the young people told us, "He's a strange man, he's not what he seems." Di Burgess, the program's researcher, found newspaper cuttings about Gleaves—he had committed sexual offences as a young man. Then we heard that he physically and sexually abused some of the young people he picked up at the stations. But just as we concluded there was no real hard evidence, one young man was murdered. That dramatically changed the nature of the film. Gleaves and two or three wardens were arrested, although Gleaves was not charged. We found ourselves filming the background to a murder case, and not the social affairs documentary about the runaway kids that we had started with.

*Johnny Go Home* exposed Gleaves. He got a four-year prison term for grievous bodily harm and buggery. While in prison he studied law and, when released, he sued a number of people—journalists, the prison authorities, and, as we had made the documentary, he took out 13 lawsuits against us. One case worked its way through the legal system, so that we had to stand trial at the Old Bailey, the UK's number one court. So it was a very edgy three weeks! If found guilty, we faced imprisonment. Fortunately he was seen for what he was—an individual with a string of convictions, rather skilfully using the legal process to get revenge on those who made a documentary that resulted in his imprisonment.

Ethical issues are very important in documentaries—after all, you are playing with people's lives. A fundamental ethical issue is to do with your relationship with the subjects in the film.

What rights do they have to change their mind once filming has begun? What responsibilities do you have to care for them afterwards? They've allowed you into their world, been exposed to the scrutiny of millions of viewers, and this can have an enormous impact on them. There is an ethical issue to do with accuracy. There have been documentaries over the last ten years where, in the interests of making films more exciting, elements have been invented; that's a grievous sin. You've got to be seen to be honest, accurate, and fair, otherwise you're on a slippery downward slope. But I don't think you can be objective in a documentary. Every frame you shoot, every decision you make about a camera angle, every cut you make in the edit, is personal. It is a journey of discovery. What you say to the audience is, "Here's what happened to me, here's what I've found, here's what I've seen, here's the story I am interpreting for you." Any documentary is inevitably a partial view.

During the making of *Rampton—The Secret Hospital* I experienced political pressure from both the Conservative and Labour parties. A Labour Member of Parliament went utterly ballistic, saying he was going to drag my name through the courts. On another occasion a Conservative MP denounced me publicly on television. Fortunately, the journalistic culture I worked in was robust enough to reject attempts to undermine my work. There was a period of intense political censorship centred around work on Northern Ireland. *Death on the Rock*, which dealt with the British Army's SAS shooting of IRA suspects on the streets of Gibraltar, became a major political issue, and there were desperate attempts by government to prevent transmission. Sometimes the consequences on

filmmakers were very, very serious. But these days I think there are other, hidden forms of censorship. One is self-censorship—filmmakers edit controversy out. Difficult programs just don't happen. The other is censorship of the bland—the drive to have programs homogenous, easy on the eye and brain. Not how you'd normally think of censorship, but it is part of the culture. If you want the next commission, or your small independent production company to survive, better not to rock the boat. Better to make the bland programs that so many broadcasters seem to want.

Conversely, pressure from advertisers was very limited. Now I think commercial pressure is much more intense. The primary motivation of broadcasters in the UK today is to maximize ratings and revenue. And there's a great deal of commercial pressure to make money out of programs through international sales, merchandising, and so on. The idea that you might be making worthwhile programs is very much a secondary factor. Social-issue documentaries, of the kind I specialized in, hardly exist on television any more. Big issues feature in drama-documentaries. Racism gets dealt with in a dramatized documentary like that of Stephen Lawrence, the young man killed in a racist attack in south London. Or two dramas about events in Londonderry on "Bloody Sunday," which had more impact than the documentary I was executive producer on. I think the drama-documentary is a valuable tool to air important and powerful issues; but it has to be properly labeled so the viewer understands which part is based on, for example, transcripts of a court case, and what is the writer's imagination. But I don't think documentary necessarily needs to entertain.

Audiences sometimes turn to documentary for a learning experience or political analysis. Of course, through making people laugh you can reveal a great deal of truth. So engaging with the audience is crucial; making documentaries that no one watches is soul-destroying. However, one of the exciting things about documentary today is that anything is possible. Young documentary makers have a whole range of influences that I never had. I was influenced by the observational documentary and current affairs journalism. I mixed the techniques so as to make a connection between crime and social problems. Young filmmakers can break rules because rules are often created by the technology available—different technology and different influences mean you can jump boundaries. If you can find the funding (and that's another matter), it's an exciting time to be making documentary.

Television is a way of exploring society. But, to be frank, I am becoming dispirited with it as a medium. There is a kind of uniformity, a formulaic quality about a great deal of especially British television that is devaluing the documentary—a tradition going back to the '30s. There are very few documentary strands left now. There are still lots of documentary hours but the regular strands, for example, *Cutting Edge* or *First Tuesday*, scarcely exist. They were the places where an editor of a strand with 20 hours a year could take a risk with new filmmakers, or make some experimental programs. Now every documentary has to get the ratings, and risk taking is being squeezed out.

*Alice—A Fight for Life*, 1982

*The Chinese Geordie*, 1983

Top: *Windscale: The Nuclear Laundry*, 1983

Above: *The Chinese Geordie*, 1983

Top and above: *From the Cradle to the Grave*, 1987

Top and above: *Rampton–The Secret Hospital*, 1979

# Interview

# Anne Regitze Wivel

15

### An introduction

Awarded a Prix Special by Frederick Wiseman for her film *David or Goliath*, Anne Wivel bemoans the low standard of the portrayal of "reality" on television, which she thinks is dominated by journalists too close to the interests that control money and power. Wivel considers that storytellers who dare to have the courage to go against powerful institutions in society will always be needed, because reality is more than just the news stories. Wivel is chairperson of the board of Barok Films, her own production company. Compelling and passionate in her documentary making, she is not only a highly regarded director, both in her native Denmark and internationally, but is also a well-respected teacher.

# Anne Regitze Wivel

*Copenhagen, September 4, 2002*

My family background is just like that of the characters in Ingmar Bergman's film *Fanny and Alexander*. I grew up in a bourgeois family house north of Copenhagen, and my father was a poet. There were always a lot of visitors; business people, artists. Mine was a mixed Jewish-Danish family—not religious but passionate, intelligent people. I feel privileged to have had this background. My father was opposed to the business side of the family. After the Second World War he formed a group whose members wrote poetry and published a magazine that had a big influence on the cultural life of Denmark.

In 1968 I went to the Royal Academy of Arts in Copenhagen to be a painter, but so many things were happening outside that I felt trapped in the academic tradition. Everything seemed to be happening elsewhere. But in the latter part of my education, I met Professor Albert Merz, a wonderful man inspired by Nam Juke Paik, the Japanese video artist. He started using video—something quite new, and I was one of the first in Denmark who took up the medium. Together with Merz, I shot a lot of video. I was interested in what was out in the streets. At the time I didn't call it documentary, but in fact it was. So I became a documentary maker. What we produced was not shown in cinemas but in galleries—it was kind of avant-garde thinking. That was my beginning.

We students felt our work was very experimental, but when we returned to the Academy another professor, Helge Bertram, also a man I admired very much, reviewed our material with us and taught us to look at it in a formal way. So I learnt about framing, composition, and perspective, and about European ways of building images. One approach is to construct a picture by understanding how the shapes are formed; the other approach is based on colors forming the picture. This is like leaving a room in which only one source of light forms shadows, and outside you suddenly see colors. Two very different approaches, which were both very interesting for me. I'm the sort of person who leaves the room and looks at the colors—like an Impressionist. It's my background.

I'm interested in reality—in telling stories about reality. I appreciate good journalism, and maybe I could have been a journalist, but I wanted to make documentaries. After the Academy I went to the National Film School of Denmark. It was one of the first in Europe. I was five years older than most of the other students. I'm always the oldest. It's my privilege. Now I'm very close to the school and still teach there. The documentary maker Jørgen Leth was not at the same film school, but he often visited, and we watched his films. He was like a big brother, and his ideas were very inspiring. I didn't want to work in the same way as him, but his work meant a lot to me and also to a lot of other people.

When I was young I was very shy. In my big family, everybody was always talking. I only listened, and I think in many ways it was very good, but it was also painful not having the courage to express myself. I was a good painter and painted a lot, but it was lonely and painful for me to be so alone. So when I got video in my hands, suddenly I was able to do things with other people. Suddenly I had access to others, and a good excuse for having other people near me.

*Greenland*, currently in production

*Greenland*, currently in production

*Greenland*, currently in production

I have recently worked with a new group of people on a film called *Greenland*. But for many years I have been making films with the same photographer, the same editor, often the same sound person. Many of them are friends from the film school. Ghita Beckendorff is the editor on a lot of my films. She's a very important person for me. My films tend to run for about 100 minutes or so. So we're in the editing suite together for 10 or 12 weeks—we know each other very well. *Greenland* is in 35mm for cinema, but it is made in many formats—8- and 16mm-film and video.

Greenland is a Danish colony. I wanted to tell a very personal story; my story about Greenland. It is never described as I see it—as a modern country with a history and many problems. The country is more than just its wonderful nature, more than just the country of the poor drunken Greenlanders— it is a society of decent, clever people. Starting this summer, and continuing for the next 12 months, I will follow the political process in Greenland. The Greenlanders are struggling to have more autonomy. In this film I wanted to recall the work of the Danish documentary maker Jørgen Roos, who made wonderful black-and-white films of Greenland. It is not a cheap film, and I tried for some years to get the money for the project. In the end I received a lot of support from both the fiction and documentary departments of the Danish Film Institute, I also got finance from the European MEDIA fund, backing from various Scandinavian sources, and a pre-sale to Danish and other Nordic television stations.

It is increasingly difficult to raise funding because television has more and more power, and television executives don't particularly respect documentary. But I will not compromise my ideas after so many years in this business, so it is not easy. In Denmark, I think it's almost impossible to make a film without television involvement. You have to have television with you, but it is not of utmost importance. The country has a law that states film should be regarded as art, so we can go to the Film Institute and say, "Now listen, this project is art." But if you secure a television sale, then it's easier to get money from the Institute.

I have a small production company within the Nordic Film Company, and right now we have 30 projects on the go. I go to the Film Institute with young directors and talk about their ideas, and tell the Institute what idiots they are if they don't fund this or that project. Now I am able to do a lot for younger colleagues, and it's very inspiring for me. I will never give up making films independently, but I do devote two days a week to my company.

Many of my films have won prizes abroad and have been released in other countries. In 1994 I made a three-hour film on the Danish philosopher Søren Kierkegaard, which was translated into five languages and is the only film ever made about him. Back in 1988 I made *David or Goliath*—a 107-minute film about the World Press in Jerusalem. It was just when the first Intifada started. I was there as a journalist for an independent newspaper in Denmark. At the press building in Jerusalem the Israeli spokesman had a hard time explaining what was going on. He was such a passionate man that I was suddenly reminded of Frederick Wiseman; I then saw this building and this man as the center of a documentary. I returned to Denmark and explained my idea to the Institute, and got the money very quickly. In April 1988 I was back in Jerusalem with a small crew, and in three weeks we had shot a film in this press building, reflecting what was going on through journalists from all over the world, and this Israeli spokesman trying to deal with them. It was the first time in Israel's history that they stopped the press from going to the front lines. I followed this issue as it was taken to the Israeli High Court—a dramatic time for the country. *David or Goliath* was seen at many festivals. Wiseman was on one jury, and he gave me the Prix Special at the Filmer à Tout Prix, in Brussels. I was so happy to get a prize from him.

I feel that the video camera is now like a pencil with which to sketch. I can make wonderful pictures with this camera, and, in fact, I have made two long films with myself as the photographer. I like to make video notes; it is like being a painter again. But with *Greenland* I try to incorporate video into film, and black and white with color, because I want to layer the story. At one level it is about a young politician who is a key figure in Greenland. He is a member of the parliament in Copenhagen for Greenland, and I follow him with my little video camera. Then there will be a lot of portraits of Greenlanders in black and white.

At the editing stage, many of my films have been cut on a Steinbeck. Now they are all done on Avid, and I work alone with the editor. Not so long ago, there was an assistant, people came from the laboratory—there were always people coming and going from the cutting room. Now we are in this silent room with all these buttons and screens. The editor is more like a doctor. She is not the same editor, and I am not the same director. In the old days we had to imagine what the edit or effect would be like when it came back from the laboratory after several days. Now we see what we are thinking at the touch of a button.

I come from a tradition of producing for the big screen. The best way to see a film is in the cinema in a dark room. But it's important that it be seen on television, too. I am very interested in close-ups, although *Greenland* is in wide-screen format. Faces tell you so much when they are not talking. I like to look at people listening, to see how they are feeling. However, I have never used interviews. People talk a lot in my films, but they are not interviewed. I try to place people who really have something to say to each other in pressured situations. For example, in *David or Goliath* people had so much to say and expressed so much with body language; it was obviously from the heart. I love this temperament. It's a Jewish trait that I know from my family.

Before shooting, I talk with the participants and explain that every human being has conflicts, and that I want to record those conflicts. I don't think a conflict is a private thing, it's for everybody to share. If I manage to get their agreement, they're always very willing and give openly. I made a film about a wonderful old ballet master at the Royal Theater in Denmark, *Giselle—A Film about Dream and Discipline* on 35mm in black and white. It was the most beautiful film I have made. But there was a lot of conflict in it. The documentary followed the process of setting up a big romantic ballet, and the principal character was this aging ballet master who had danced the main part himself as a young man. I told him that I saw him as melancholy—sometimes depressed, sometimes happy. I find that if I tell people how I see them they say, "You are right! You are right!" Then they act in a suitably melancholic way. But you must be very honest and only tell them what you as the director see. I never use my status as a woman, never flirt or anything, to gain advantage of someone. Instead, I let people know that I suffer from shyness. I find they are sympathetic to this, and frequently we become close friends.

My films are a subjective statement. In *Greenland* I shall attempt to use commentary, which will be the first time in my life that I've done so. I also write poetry, but have never wanted to use it in my films. However, I did experiment by using my own voice while operating the camera in *The Castle in Italy*, which I made in 2000. A friend and well-known Danish artist, Per Kirkeby, painter, geologist, and poet, was going through a depression. His marriage was falling apart. He was about 55 at the time. I was there for a week with another friend Ib Michael, also a poet. My film is an attempt to capture three old friends (one of whom was me, always off-camera) in this Italian castle working through Per's life crisis. It was a fantastic film that took a long time to edit.

Although I don't dramatize exactly, I do direct. I'm not so concerned about the distinction between fiction and documentary, as I know all too well how much we manipulate situations. I think I have a responsibility to trust my feelings and what I am really interested in. I never try to hide behind some falsity, some deceit. Just as I don't hide the fact that I think it's entertaining to be informed, and that I want people to feel good about my work. I believe in talking to the brain and the heart, and reminding people that it's wonderful to listen to something intelligent and fantastic, because a lot of documentary is about people's stupidity, and that doesn't interest me. So I've learnt the lesson to trust my feelings and my own stupidity, and to look within myself and the participants of my films. Then I remain with just one ambition—to continue.

Anne Wivel on location
*Søren Kierkegaard*, 1994

*Greenland*, currently in production

# In the end…

whatever the prevailing political or cultural circumstance in which the documentary is made, all directors are faced with the same ethical question—where lies the border between the journalistic and the artistic? How far from the straight and narrow can the documentary maker wander into the realms of the "creative treatment of actuality" before getting lost in the land of fakery? While all here agree that documentary is not fiction, they vary in degree as to the extent that documentary must be reality. Without a license to interpret life as they see it, what future can there be for the documentary? To what degree is it acceptable to intervene? *Cinéma vérité* has been overtaken by other forms purporting to have the same "hands off" validity—direct cinema, fly-on-the-wall, reality television. But each, in its own way, bears the same weakness of subjectivity—where on the wall to place the camera, and where in the take to make the cut?

Now there is a new kid on the block who goes by the name of factual programing. He and his kind struggle with their own set of ethical issues imposed by the rigidity of their name. The documentary suffers no such constraints and remains at large, healthy, and active. Long live the documentary!

# Acknowledgements

It was no easy task to locate and interview, across four continents, the documentary makers here. Were it not for the generous assistance of so many whose interests were simply to see this book into print, I would still be at it—I am truly indebted to you all, as indeed I am to the documentary makers themselves, from whom I have learnt so much.

For your kindness and assistance, thank you…
Arne Bro, National Film School of Denmark
Chris Berry, University of California
Judith Burns, The Home Office
Elaine and Jacques Carteau, Barbizon
Silvano Cavatora, FILMMAKER
Susanna Chivian, WGBH TV
Fred Gehler, Dokfestival-Leipzig
Gabriel Hall, Zweites Deutsches Fernsehen
Kathy Loizou (then), Sheffield International Documentary Festival
Sally Ingleton, Sydney
Karoline Leth, National Film School of Denmark
Diane Masciotra, National Film Board of Canada
Francis Kendal, Planet TV
Renate Sachse, Paris
Keith Shiri, Centre for African Film
Brian Winston, University of Westminster

A special thanks to Merry Kemp and Derek Roe for your fluency in translation.

I reserve a particular acknowledgement to this book's editor, Erica ffrench. From the very beginning to the very last, your support, encouragement, and above all, wisdom, has been its making.

And by no means least, a final word of appreciation to Mariolina, for your tireless support and enthusiasm throughout these most challenging months.

# Picture credits

p8–19 Courtesy of Florentine Films/Ken Burns p20–21 Copyright Fergus Greer p23–24 Courtesy of Molly Dineen p25 Courtesy of Minotaur p27 Courtesy of Molly Dineen p28–31 Copyright Nick Danzigger/Contact/NB Pictures p32–35 Copyright Ben Osborne/naturepl.com p36 Copyright Doug Allan/ naturepl.com p37–39 Copyright Sue Flood/naturepl.com p40 Copyright Klaus Nigge/naturepl.com p41 Courtesy of Alastair Fothergill p42 (left) Copyright Doug Allan/naturepl.com (middle, right) Copyright Sue Flood/naturepl.com p43 Copyright Sue Flood/naturepl.com p44–45 Copyright Ekko von Schwichow, courtesy of ZDF/Hans-Dieter Grabe p47–53 Copyright ZDF/Hans-Dieter Grabe p54–63 Courtesy of Patricio Guzmán p64–65, 67 Courtesy of Bonnie Sherr Klein p68 Courtesy of and photo by Dorothy Todd Hénaut p69 (left) Courtesy of Dorothy Todd Hénaut, photo by Guy Borremans, (right) photo used with permission of the National Film Board of Canada p71 Courtesy of Bonnie Sherr Klein p72–73 Photos used with permission of the National Film Board of Canada p74–75, 77–80 Courtesy of Cabin Creek Films/ Barbara Kopple p82–83 Courtesy of Barbara Kopple, copyright Fine Line Features p85 Courtesy of Cabin Creek Films/Barbara Kopple p86–87, 89–93 Courtesy of Nordisk Film/Jørgen Leth p94–95 Courtesy of Nordisk Film/Jørgen Leth, photos by Dan Holmberg p96–97 Courtesy of Globe Department Store/Errol Morris, photo by Nubar Alexanian p98 Courtesy of Globe Department Store/Errol Morris, photo by John Giannini p99 Courtesy of Globe Department Store/Errol Morris, photos by Mark Lipson p100–01 Courtesy of Globe Department Store/Errol Morris, photos by John Giannini p102 Courtesy of Globe Department Store/Errol Morris, photos by Nubar Alexanian p103 Courtesy of Globe Department Store/Errol Morris, photo by Rosalie Winard p104–05 Courtesy of Globe Department Store/Errol Morris, photos by Nubar Alexanian p106–15 Courtesy of Anand Patwardhan p116–25 Courtesy of Jean-Marie Teno, copyright Les Films du Raphia p126–27 Courtesy of the Royal Television Society p129–31 Copyright BBC p132 Copyright Channel Four, photo by Gisele Wulfsohn p134–35 Copyright Channel Four, photos by Rachel Joseph p136–37 Copyright BBC p138–39 Courtesy of Wu Wenguang, photo by Lin Yuojuan p140 Courtesy of Wu Wenguang p141 Courtesy of Wu Wenguang, photo by Lin Yuojuan p142–45, 147 Courtesy of Wu Wenguang p148–49 Courtesy of WGBH Boston p151–53 Copyright Granada Media. Disclaimer—RotoVision indemnifies Granada Media from responsibility for this image (p153) p155–57 Copyright Granada Media p158–67 Courtesy of Anne Regitze Wivel

# Further information

## Books

Barnouw, E. *Documentary: A History of the Non-Fiction Film*. Oxford University Press, 1976.

Bell, E. *The Origins of British Television Documentary: The BBC 1946–1955*. 1986.

Brianzoli, G, Chatrian, C, & Mosso, L. *Paesaggi Umani: Il Cinema di Frederick Wiseman*. Filmmaker, 2000.

Corner, J., ed. *The Art of Record: A Critical Introduction to Documentary*. Manchester University Press, 1996.

*Documentaries: The Independents' Guide*. BBC, 1994.

Grierson, J. *Grierson on Documentary*. Faber & Faber, 1946.

*Guidelines for Factual Programmes*. BBC, 1989.

Kilborn, R & Izod, J. *Confronting Reality: An Introduction to Television Documentary*. Manchester University Press, 1997.

Kriwaczek, P. *Documentary for the Small Screen*. Focal Press, 1997.

Levin, G Roy. *Documentary Explorations: Fifteen Interviews with Filmmakers*. Doubleday, 1971.

Macdonald, K & Cousins, M. *Imagining Reality: The Faber Book of the Documentary*. Faber & Faber, 1997.

*Producers' Guidelines*. BBC, 1993.

Rabiger, M. *Directing the Documentary*. Focal Press, 1997.

Rosenthal, A. *The Documentary Conscience : A Casebook in Film Making*. University of California Press, 1980.

Rosenthal, A. *New Challenges for Documentary*. University of California Press, 1988.

Rosenthal, A. *The New Documentary in Action: A Casebook in Film Making*. University of California Press, 1971.

Rosenthal, A. *Writing, Directing, and Producing Documentary Films and Videos*. Southern Illinois University Press, 1990.

Rotha, P. *Documentary Film*. Faber & Faber, 1939.

Silverstone, R. *Framing Science: The Making of a BBC Documentary*. British Film Institute, 1985.

Stenderup, T., ed. *The European Documentary Sector*. MEDIA Copenhagen, 1995.

Stephenson, R. & Debrix, J. R. *The Cinema as Art*. Penguin, 1966.

Tobias, M., ed. *The Search for Reality: The Art of Documentary Filmmaking*. Michael Wiese Productions, 1998.

## Journals

*doc waves*
Documentary making in the UK
www.filmwaves.co.uk

*DOX*
Journal of the European Documentary Network
www.dox.dk

*FILMMAKER*
Publication of the International Festival of Cinema and Video
www.filmmakermagazine.com

*International Documentary*
Magazine of the International Documentary Association
www.documentary.org

# Festivals

Academia Film Olomouc, Czech Republic
www.afo.cz

Amnesty International Film Festival, Amsterdam
www.amnesty.nl/filmfestival

Australian International Documentary Conference
www.aidc.com.au

Chicago International Doc Film Festival, USA
www.chicagodocfestival.org

Cinéma du Réel, France
www.bpi.fr

Cracow Film Festival, Poland
www.cracowfilmfestival.pl

Denver Jazz on Film Festival, USA
www.jazzfilmfestival.org

Diagonale, Austria
www.diagonale.at

Docaviv International Documentary Film Festival, Israel
www.docaviv.co.il

docfest : New York International Documentary Festival, USA
www.docfest.org

Doclands, Ireland
www.doclands.ie

DocSide Film Festival, USA
e-mail: docfilmproject@excite.com

DoubleTake Documentary Film Festival, USA
www.ddff.org

Doxa: Documentary Film and Video Festival, Canada
www.vcn.bc.ca/doxa

Edinburgh International Film Festival, UK
www.edfilmfest.org.uk

États Généraux du film Documentaire, France
www.lussasdoc.com

Fairfax Documentary Film Festival, USA
e-mail: weinsoff@ix.netcom.com

Festival dei Popoli, Italy
www.festivaldeipopoli.org

Festival International du Documentaire de Marseille, France
www.fidmarseille.org

Hot Docs Canadian International Documentary Festival
www.hotdocs.ca

The Hot Springs Documentary Film Festival, USA
www.docufilminst.org

Human Rights Watch International Film Festival, UK/USA
www.hrw.org

Infinity Festival, Italy
www.infinityfestival.org

INPUT 2003, Denmark
www.input2003.com

International 1001 Documentary Film Festival, Turkey
www.bsb-adf.org

International Documentary Film Festival, Amsterdam
www.idfa.nl

International Documentary Film Festival (DOCtober), USA
www.documentary.org/festivals

International Film Festival on Human Rights, Switzerland
www.fifdh.ch

International Short Film Festival Oberhausen, Germany
www.kurzfilmtage.de

Iowa City International Documentary Film Festival, USA
www.icdocs.org

It's All True International Documentary Film Festival, Brazil
www.itsalltrue.com.br

Jackson Hole Wildlife Film Festival, USA
www.jhfestival.org

Karlovy Vary International Film Festival, Czech Republic
www.iffkv.cz

Lisbon Docs, Portugal
e-mail: fidl@clix.pt

Margaret Mead Film & Video Festival, USA
www.amnh.org/mead

Melbourne International Film Festival, Australia
www.melbournefilmfestival.com.au

Message To Man, Russia
www.message-to-man.spb.ru

MIPDOC, France
www.mipdoc.com

Munich International Documentary Film Festival, Germany
www.dokfestival-muenchen.de

The Museum of Television & Radio's Television Documentary
Festival, USA
www.mtr.org/tvdocfest

NatFilm Festivalen, Denmark
www.natfilm.dk

New Zealand International Film Festivals
www.enzedff.co.nz

Odense International Film Festival, Denmark
www.filmfestival.dk

One World International Human Rights Film Festival, Czech Republic
www.oneworld.cz

Pärnu International Documentary & Anthropology Film Festival,
Estonia
www.chaplin.ee

queerdoc, Australia
www.queerscreen.com.au

RAI International Festival of Ethnographic Film, UK
www.therai.org.uk

San Francisco International Film Festival, USA
www.sfiff.org

São Paolo International Short Film Festival, Brazil
www.kinoforum.org

Sheffield International Documentary Festival, UK
www.sidf.co.uk

Silverdocs, USA
www.silverdocs.com

Spanish Film Festival of Málaga, Spain
www.festcinemalaga.com

Sunny Side of the Doc, France
www.sunnysideofthedoc.com

Thessaloniki Documentary Festival, Greece
www.docfestival.gr

United Nations Association Film Festival, USA
www.unaff.org

Venice International Film Festival, Italy
www.labiennale.org

Visions du Réel, Switzerland
www.visionsdureel.ch

Yamagata International Documentary Film Festival, Japan
www.city.yamagata.yamagata.jp/yidff/home-e.html

ZIFF–Festival of the Dhow Countries, Zanzibar
www.ziff.or.tz

# Filmographies

Only those documentaries directed or co-directed

### Ken Burns

| | |
|---|---|
| Mark Twain | 2002 |
| Jazz, A History of America's | 2001 |
| Music (series of 10) | |
| Not for Ourselves Alone: | 1999 |
| The Story of Elizabeth Cady | |
| Stanton and Susan B Anthony | |
| Frank Lloyd Wright | 1998 |
| Thomas Jefferson | 1997 |
| Lewis and Clark: The Journey | 1997 |
| of the Corps of Discovery | |
| Vezelay | 1996 |
| The West | 1996 |
| Baseball | 1994 |
| William Segal | 1992 |
| Empire of the Air: | 1991 |
| The Men Who Made Radio | |
| The Civil War (series of 9) | 1990 |
| The Congress: | 1988 |
| The History and Promise of | |
| Representative Government | |
| Thomas Hart Benton | 1988 |
| Statue of Liberty | 1985 |
| Huey Long | 1985 |
| The Shakers: Hands to Work, | 1984 |
| Hearts to God | |
| Brooklyn Bridge | 1981 |

### Molly Dineen

| | |
|---|---|
| The Lords' Tale | 2002 |
| Geri | 1999 |
| Tony Blair | 1997 |
| In the Company of Men | 1995 |
| The Ark | 1993 |
| The Pick, The Shovel and | 1990 |
| the Open Road | |
| Heart of the Angel | 1989 |
| My African Farm | 1988 |
| Operation Raleigh: The Mountain | 1988 |
| Operation Raleigh: The Village | 1988 |
| Home from the Hill | 1985 |
| Sound Business | n/a |

### Alastair Fothergill

| | |
|---|---|
| Planet Earth (working title) | tba |
| The Blue Planet | 1998–2001 |
| (directed 3 of 8) | |
| An Island All Alone | 1997 |
| Life in the Freezer (series of 6) | 1992–93 |
| Too Close for Comfort | 1991 |
| The Trials of Life (series of 12) | 1990 |
| Reef Watch (live broadcast) | 1988 |
| The Really Wild Show | 1985–97 |

### Hans-Dieter Grabe

| | |
|---|---|
| These Pictures Haunt Me– | 2002 |
| Alfred Jahn, M.D. (*Diese Bilder* | |
| *verfolgen mich –Dr.med.Alfred Jahn*) | |
| Broken Glow–My Visits with | 2001 |
| Jürgen Böttcher (*Gebrochene Glut*) | |
| Mendel is Alive (*Mendel Lebt*) | 1999 |
| Do Sanh–The Last Film | 1998 |
| (*Do Sanh–Der Letzte Film*) | |
| Poddembice–A Documentary | 1996 |
| Trilogy (*Poddembice–eine* | |
| *Dokumentarische Trilogie*) | |
| He Called Himself Hohenstein | 1994 |
| (*Er Nannte sich Hohenstein*) | |
| Do Sanh | 1991 |
| Dien, Chinh, Chung and Tung– | 1990 |
| Struggling to Live in Vietnam again | |
| (*Dien, Chinh, Chung und Tung–* | |
| *Lebensversuche in Vietnam*) | |
| Abdullah Yakupoglü: "Why Did I | 1986 |
| Kill My Daughter?" (*Abdullah* | |
| *Yakupoglü: "Warum habe ich meine* | |
| *Tochter getötet?"*) | |
| I Plead Guilty–Lew Kopelew | 1986 |
| (*Ich Bekenne mich Schuldig–* | |
| *Lew Kopelew*) | |
| Hiroshima, Nagasaki–Nuclear | 1985 |
| Bomb Victims Testify | |
| (*Hiroshima, Nagasaki–* | |
| *Atombombenopfer segen aus*) | |
| Alfred Jahn, M.D., Pediatric | 1984 |
| Surgeon (*Dr. med. Alfred Jahn–* | |
| *Kinderchirurg in Landshut*) | |
| Ludwig Gehm | 1983 |
| Workers from Dantzig | 1982 |
| (*Arbeiter aus Dantzig*) | |
| Bernauer Strasse 1-50 Or When | 1981 |
| Our Front Door was Nailed Up | |
| (*Bernauer Strasse 1-50 oder Als uns* | |
| *die Haustür zugenagelt wurde*) | |
| Mendel Szajnfeld's Second | 1971 |
| Journey to Germany (*Mendel* | |
| *Szajnfeld's Zweite Reise nach* | |
| *Deutschland*) | |
| Only Light Skirmishes in the Da | 1971 |
| Nang Area (*Nur Leichte Kampfe* | |
| *im Raum Da Nang*) | |
| 20 Miles to Saigon | 1970 |
| (*20 Meilen vor Saigon*) | |
| The Women who Cleared Away | 1968 |
| the Ruins of Berlin | |
| (*Die Trümmerfrauen von Berlin*) | |

For a more exhaustive filmography email:
internationaleprogrammkoordination@
zdf.de

## Patricio Guzmán

| | |
|---|---|
| Madrid | 2002 |
| The Pinochet Case | 2000 |
| (*Le Cas Pinochet*) | |
| Robinson Crusoe Island | 1999 |
| Obstinate Memory | 1997 |
| (*Chile, la Memoria Obstinada*) | |
| The Barriers of Loneliness | 1995 |
| Southern Cross | 1989–92 |
| (*La Cruz del Sur*, series of 4) | |
| In the Name of God | 1987 |
| (*En Nombre de Dios*) | |
| Precolombian Mexico | 1985 |
| (series of 5) | |
| The Battle of Chile | 1973–79 |
| (*La Batalla de Chile*, series of 3) | |
| The First Year | 1971 |
| (*Primer Año*) | |

## Bonnie Sherr Klein

| | |
|---|---|
| Mile Zero: The SAGE Tour | 1988 |
| Children of War | 1987 |
| Speaking Our Peace | 1985 |
| Not a Love Story | 1981 |
| (*C'est Surtout pas de l'Amour*) | |
| The Right Candidate for Rosedale | 1979 |
| Patricia's Moving Picture | 1978 |
| Harmonie | 1977 |
| A Working Chance | 1976 |
| (*Du Coeur... l'Ouvrage*) | |
| Citizens' Medicine | 1970 |
| (*Clinique des Citoyens*) | |
| VTR St Jacques | 1970 |
| (*Opération Boule de Neige*) | |
| Little Burgundy | 1968 |
| Organizing for Power: | 1968 |
| The Alinsky Approach | |
| (series of 5) | |
| For All My Students | 1966 |

## Barbara Kopple

| | |
|---|---|
| American Standoff | 2002 |
| Conversations with Gregory Peck | 2000 |
| Kids and Learning Disabilities | 2000 |
| My Generation | 2000 |
| Friends for Life | 1999 |
| Defending Our Daughters | 1998 |
| Wild Man Blues | 1997 |
| A Century of Women | 1994 |
| Fallen Champ: | 1993 |
| The Untold Story of Mike Tyson | |
| Beyond JFK: | 1992 |
| The Question of Conspiracy | |
| American Dream | 1990 |
| Hurricane Irene | 1985 |
| No Nukes | 1981 |
| Harlan County, USA | 1976 |

## Jørgen Leth

| | |
|---|---|
| The Five Obstructions | tba |
| The Erotic Human (working title) | tba |
| New Scenes from America | 2002 |
| (*Nye Scener fra Amerika*) | |
| I'm Alive. Soren Ulrik Thomsen: | 1999 |
| A Danish Poet | |
| (*Jeg er Levende–Soren Ulrik Thomsen, Digter*) | |
| Haïti. Untitled (*Haïti. Uden titel*) | 1996 |
| Michael Laudrup: A Football | 1993 |
| Player (*Michael Laudrup–en Fodboldspiller*) | |
| Notes on Love | 1989 |
| (*Notater om Kærligheden*) | |
| Danish Literature | 1989 |
| (*Dansk Litteratur*) | |
| Notebook from China | 1987 |
| (*Notater fra Kina*) | |
| Composer Meets Quartet | 1987 |
| Moments of Play | 1986 |
| (*Det Legende Menneske*) | |
| Pelota | 1983 |
| 66 Scenes from America | 1982 |
| (*66 Scener fra Amerika*) | |
| Step on Silence | 1981 |
| Peter Martins: A Dancer | 1979 |
| (*Peter Martins–en Danser*) | |
| Kalule | 1979 |
| Dancing Bournonville | 1979 |
| (*At Danse Bournonville*) | |
| A Midsummer's Play | 1979 |
| (*Sanct Hansaften-Spil*) | |
| A Sunday in Hell | 1977 |
| (*En Forårsdag i Helvede*) | |
| Good and Evil | 1975 |
| (*Det Gode og det Onde*) | |
| Klaus Rifbjerg | 1975 |
| The Impossible Hour | 1975 |
| (*Den Umulige Time*) | |
| Stars and Watercarriers | 1974 |
| (*Stjernerne og Vandbærerne*) | |
| Eddy Merckx in the Vicinity | 1973 |
| of a Cup of Coffee | |
| (*Eddy Merckx i Nærheden af en Kop Kaffe*) | |
| Life in Denmark (*Livet i Danmark*) | 1972 |
| Chinese Ping Pong | 1972 |
| (*Kinesisk Bordtennis*) | |
| The Search (*Eftersøgningen*) | 1971 |
| Without Ken (*Frændeløs*) | 1970 |
| The Deer Garden, The Romantic | 1970 |
| Forest (*Dyrehaven, den Romantiske Skov*) | |
| Motion Picture | 1970 |
| The Theater of the | 1970 |
| Green Mountains | |
| (*Teatret il de Grønne Bjerge*) | |
| The Deer Garden Film | 1969 |
| (*Dyrehavefilmen*) | |
| Jens Otto Krag | 1969 |
| The Perfect Human | 1968 |
| (*Det Perfekte Menneske*) | |
| Near Heaven, Near Earth | 1968 |
| (*Nær Himlen, Nær Jorden*) | |
| Ophelia's Flowers | 1968 |
| (*Ofelias Blomster*) | |
| Look Forward to a | 1965 |
| Time of Security | |
| (*Se Frem til en Tryg Tid*) | |
| Stop for Bud (*Stopforbud*) | 1963 |

## Errol Morris

| | |
|---|---|
| Mr Death: The Rise and Fall | 1999 |
| of Fred A Leuchter Jnr | |
| Stairway to Heaven | 1998 |
| Fast, Cheap, and Out of Control | 1996 |
| A Brief History of Time | 1992 |
| The Thin Blue Line | 1988 |
| Vernon, Florida | 1981 |
| Gates of Heaven | 1977 |

## Anand Patwardhan

| | |
|---|---|
| War and Peace (*Jang aur Aman*) | 2002 |
| We are Not Your Monkeys | 1996 |
| (*Nahi Amhi Vanar Bannar*) | |
| Fishing: In the Sea of Greed | 1998 |
| Occupation: Millworker | 1996 |
| A Narmada Diary | 1996 |
| Father, Son and Holy War | 1995 |
| (*Pitra Putra aur Dharmayuddha*) | |
| In the Name of God | 1992 |
| (*Raam ke Naam*) | |
| In Memory of Friends | 1990 |
| (*Una Mitran di Yaad Pyaari*) | |
| Bombay Our City | 1985 |
| (*Hamar Shahar*) | |
| A Time to Rise (*Utthan da Vela*) | 1981 |
| Prisoners of Conscience | 1978 |
| (*Zameer ke Bandi*) | |
| Waves of Revolution | 1974 |
| (*Kranti ki Tarangen*) | |
| Business as Usual | 1971 |

## Jean-Marie Teno

| | |
|---|---|
| Alex's Wedding | 2002 |
| (*Le Mariage d'Alex*) | |
| A Trip to the Country | 2000 |
| (*Vacances au Pays*) | |
| Chief! (*Chef!*) | 1999 |
| Head in the Clouds | 1994 |
| (*La Tête dans les Nuages*) | |
| Africa, I Will Fleece You | 1992 |
| (*Afrique, je te Plumerai…*) | |
| Mister Foot | 1991 |
| Bikutsi Water Blues | 1988 |
| Homage (*Hommage*) | 1985 |
| Schubbah | 1983 |

## Paul Watson

| | |
|---|---|
| Desert Darlings (working title) | tba |
| The Queen's Wedding | 2002 |
| A Wedding in the Family | 2000 |
| Malcolm and Barbara: | 1999 |
| A Love Story | |
| White Lives | 1998 |
| The Dinner Party | 1997 |
| The Home | 1995 |
| The Factory | 1994 |
| Trick on Two | 1993 |
| Sylvania Waters (series of 12) | 1992 |
| Sarajevo 90 x 2 minutes | 1992 |
| (transmitted daily) | |
| The Fishing Party | 1985 |
| Nobody Asked Us | 1980 |
| The Family (series of 12) | 1974 |
| A Fine and Private Place | n/a |
| A Year in the Life | n/a |
| Convictions | n/a |
| House of Hope | n/a |
| In Solidarity (series of 4) | n/a |
| Lost in Space | n/a |
| Loveless in Letchworth | n/a |
| Nothing Doing | n/a |
| One Day | n/a |
| Race of the Powerbikes | n/a |
| Revelations | n/a |
| States of Mind | n/a |
| The Block | n/a |
| Vox Pop (series) | n/a |
| War in the Middle East | n/a |
| Whicker's World (series of 4) | n/a |
| Wimps to Warriors (series of 6) | n/a |

## Wu Wenguang

| | |
|---|---|
| Big Tent: Life on the Road | tba |
| (working title) | |
| Dance with the Farm Workers | 2001 |
| (*He Mingong Tiaowu*) | |
| Life on the Road (*Jiang Hu*) | 1999 |
| Diary: Snow, 21 Nov, 1998 | 1999 |
| (*Riji: Xue, 1998.11.21*) | |
| At Home in the World | 1995 |
| (*Si Hai Wei Jia*) | |
| 1966, My Time in the Red Guards | 1992 |
| (*1966, Wo De Hongweibin Shidai*) | |
| Bumming in Beijing: | 1990 |
| The Last Dreamers (*Liulang Beijing: Zuihou De Mengxiangzhe*) | |

## John Willis

| | |
|---|---|
| From the Cradle to the Grave | 1987 |
| Leftover Children | 1987 |
| Granny Business | 1987 |
| Len Harding: Born a Number | 1986 |
| Children Who Wait | 1986 |
| Churchill's Few—The Battle | 1985 |
| of Britain Remembered | |
| Families Who Wait | 1984 |
| Promised Land | 1984 |
| Place for Stephen | 1984 |
| Return to Nagasaki | 1984 |
| The Chinese Geordie | 1983 |
| Shadow Boxer | 1983 |
| Windscale: The Nuclear Laundry | 1983 |
| Alice—A Fight for Life | 1982 |
| Prisoners of Conscience | 1981 |
| Rampton—The Secret Hospital | 1979 |
| The Case of Yolande McShane | 1978 |
| Sick in Sheffield, | 1978 |
| Broke in Beverly Hills | |
| Goodbye Longfellow Road | 1977 |
| What Happened to | 1976 |
| Johnny Go Home? | |
| Johnny Go Home | 1976 |
| Whicker's World Down Under | 1976 |
| In a Monastery Garden | 1975 |
| 5 Miles High in a Hot Air Balloon | 1974 |
| Linehams of Fosdyke | 1973 |
| Charlton Brothers | 1973 |

## Anne Regitze Wivel

| | |
|---|---|
| Greenland | tba |
| (*Grønland*—working title) | |
| The Castle in Italy | 2000 |
| (*Slottet i Italien—en Elegi*) | |
| The Heart of Johannes | 1998 |
| (*Johannes' Hjerte*) | |
| Tobacco (*Tobak*) | 1996 |
| Søren Kierkegaard | 1994 |
| Giselle—A Film about Dream | 1991 |
| and Disipline | |
| Water (*Vand*) | 1988 |
| David or Goliath | 1988 |
| (*David og Goliath*) | |
| Face to Face—A Film about | 1987 |
| Faith, Hope and Love | |
| (*Ansigt til Ansigt*) | |
| The Silent Girls | 1985 |
| (*De Tavse Piger*) | |
| The Little Girl with the Skates | 1985 |
| (*Den Lille Pige med Skøjterne*) | |
| Gorilla Gorilla | 1984 |
| Motivation (*Moationtiv*) | 1983 |
| Work Towards Freedom | 1980 |
| (*Arbejde mod Frihed*) | |

# Terms used

## Terminology used by The Documentary Makers

For a more exhaustive list of terms go to
www.st-andrews.ac.uk/~roguep/rogueproductions

|  |  |
|---|---|
| 1-inch videotape | refers to the width, and implies the highest quality available at the time |
| 8, 16, or 35mm | film widths, or gauges, always expressed in millimeters, unlike **footage** |
| Animation stand | a single-frame camera mounted over a table on which stills are placed. See **Rostrum camera** |
| Arri ST | (Arriflex) 16mm film camera with three lenses, popular for many years prior to the advent of the **zoom** lens |
| Aäton | 16mm film camera, much favored by documentary makers |
| Avid | non-linear, computer-based editing system, widely used in the film and television industry |
| Batch number | used to identify unexposed film |
| Beaulieu | 16mm film camera |
| Betacam | video format |
| Black & white | film stock |
| Bolex | film camera with 8 and 16mm versions |
| Camera magazine | in which the film is loaded and attached to the camera |
| Cinéma vérité | exponents of which say it is a form that allows us to see the world as it really is |
| Color negative | film stock of any width |
| Condor | a hydrolic tower/platform also known as Simon tower, or cherry-picker |
| Cut | the simple abutting of one **shot** to another |
| Cutaway | a **shot** interposed between two segments so as to avoid a **jump-cut** |
| Cutting room | in which film is edited |
| Darkroom | in which photographs are developed |
| Dissolve | an overlapping transition between one **shot** and another |
| Dry rent | to rent equipment without a technician |
| DSR200 | a digital video camera for the consumer and semi-pro market |
| DV | digital video, as opposed to analog. A tape format for the consumer/non-pro market |
| DVCAM | as above, but runs faster than **DV** with a tougher surface coating for pro and semi-pro use |
| Eclair | 16mm camera introduced in 1960; the first hand-held **sync** camera, revolutionized documentary making |
| Emulsion | light-sensitive coating on celluloid film which, when processed, produces a negative |
| Fade | the transition from/to a blank screen |
| Flatbed | on which film is edited |
| Fps | frames per second, being the speed at which film/tape is run through a camera/projector |
| Focal length | the point at which an object is in focus |
| Footage | the material, tape or film. Film length is expressed in feet (eg: 400 ft=10mins approx) |
| Genlock | to lock a **VTR** to a synchronous signal |
| Handicam | small hand-held video camera developed for the consumer market |
| Hi-8 | an analog video tape format for the consumer/non-pro market |
| High-speed camera | shoots film at a speed which, when projected at normal speed, appears in slow-motion |
| Jump-cut | a **cut** in which the continuity of action is broken and thus has an alienating effect |
| Limbo | a setting in which there is a seamless curve between floor and wall |
| Long-shot | describes the relative size of the subject in the **shot** based on the human form |
| Narration | a superimposed voice of explanation and/or comment |
| Newsreel | a weekly news circulated in cinemas prior to the advent of television |
| Over-cranked | higher than normal camera speed |
| Pan | the horizontal movement of the camera on axis (left/right) |
| Post-production | the phase of the production process in which the editing is done |
| Premiere 6.0 | a computer-based editing system |
| Ratio | the amount of tape or film shot in relation to the final duration of the work (eg: 10:1) |
| Reversal | film **stock** which, when processed, produces a positive image |
| Rostrum camera | similar to an **animation stand** but capable of moving in relation to the table, usually computer-controlled |
| Rushes | a low-quality print rush printed to check the day's filming, also called "dailies" |
| Shot | a given length of action on film/tape |
| Steinbeck | see **Flatbed** |
| Stills | still images or photographs |
| Stock | film or tape |
| Storyboard | a series of drawings of the intended shots illustrating composition, camera angles, etc. |
| Super8 | an enhanced 8mm film format for the consumer/non-pro market |
| Sync | short for synchronous; sound recorded with the picture or edited to be synchronized with the picture |
| Talking head | euphemism for an interview done on camera |
| Tilt | the vertical movement of the camera on axis (up/down) |
| Voiceover | a voice heard over the picture and its corresponding atmosphere sounds |
| VTR | video tape recorder |
| VX1000 | a digital video camera for the consumer and semi-pro market |
| Wireless mic | microphone linked via a radio transmitter |
| Zoom | change in focal length from a wide to narrow angle, creating the illusion of movement |

# Index